XLR8

**A PROPHETIC & PRACTICAL *BLUEPRINT*
TO DOUBLE YOUR CHURCH**

MICHAEL R. MURPHY
FOUNDER OF LEADERSCAPE

AVAIL

DEDICATION

To my Lord and Savior Jesus Christ, without Whom my life would still be a mess.

To my spectacular wife, Valery. This book would not have happened without your encouragement. Your love and loyalty mean the world to me.

To our children, Leah and Andrew, Ryan and Bindi, Elyse, and our grandkids Freddie, Aubrey, Monty, and Margaux. You are our greatest joys.

To my mother and father, Valerie and Richard Murphy, who modeled sacrificial love in raising seven children, always making great memories.

To my friend and former director of Leaderscape, Anthony Richards, who, though you left us too soon, exemplified kingdom leadership with an intensity and passion rarely seen.

To our very first partners, right at the start of our Leaderscape journey ten years ago, Steve and Sharon Kelly, Rob and Becca Ketterling, and Geoff and Lee Blight. You believed in us when we were still working it all out!

To all of my friends and mentors in ministry, your support and encouragement over four decades now have kept us moving forward in life and leadership.

ACKNOWLEDGMENTS

To all our friends at AVAIL, Dr. Sam Chand, Martijn, Sarah, Debbie, Allison, and Andrew—this project has been a true partnership and it would not have happened without you.

To the amazing Pat Springle, your writing skills have brought this project to life.

To the hundreds of Lead Pastors who have engaged as partners with Leaderscape programs over the past decade. Watching you soar with new accelerated momentum is the reason we do what we do.

To our Australian Christian Churches President Wayne Alcorn and all our ACC family—walking with you and serving you over the past four decades has helped shape me more than you know.

To the Council and staff at Alphacrucis University College, especially Professor Stephen Fogarty, partnering in this generational vision has been my absolute honor.

CONTENTS

Acknowledgments . . . . *xi*

Foreword . . . . *xv*

    Formula 1 19

    Start Your Engines 33

FIX YOUR NETS 51

    First Gear: Engage Every Guest 53

    Second Gear: Explode Your Growth Track 69

FILL YOUR FUNNEL 85

    Third Gear: Max Your Sunday 87

    Fourth Gear: Mobilize for Mission 105

FUEL YOUR MULTIPLICATION 131

    Fifth Gear: Empower Your Groups 133

    Sixth Gear: Equip All Leaders 147

FLEX YOUR CAPACITY 161

    Seventh Gear: Free Your Soul 163

    Eighth Gear: Fund Your Vision 185

    Pedal to the Metal 205

About the Author *207*

For Lead Pastors Only *211*

ONE MILLION DISCIPLES 2030 215

FOREWORD

Most successful leaders have charisma.

They exude strength and energy while remaining accessible and relatable. Those led by such a leader experience both an inspirational and aspirational quality, knowing their leader understands their challenges and struggles while equipping and empowering them to reach their full potential. They trust these leaders and feel drawn to them in order to be a part of something bigger than themselves.

Effective leaders in the church are no different. Most have an appeal unique to who they are and how God made them—a humble confidence that's magnetic and contagious. They know that risks are essential to leading, serving, and walking by faith. Many such pastors and ministry leaders reach a point where they realize they have been relying on their personal charisma, charm and warmth, and humor and likability, rather than the power of the Holy Spirit to fuel their leadership style.

Realizing the performance trap they've created, these leaders tend to work harder and burn out faster—or, they surrender their egos, comparative competitive mindset, their status, and rely on true charisma—the gifts of God through His Spirit. These leaders embrace their fears even as their trust in God grows stronger and their commitment to serve the church digs deeper. They invest in everyone they encounter and give generously of their wisdom, experience, and insight. They impact other leaders and pastors with a shared sense of understanding, excitement, and fellowship. They are eager to pour into others as they overflow with all that has been poured into them.

My friend Michael Murphy embodies this kind of Christlike leader. With his brash Aussie confidence tempered by his tender shepherd's heart for others, Michael continues to invest in God's kingdom in ways that multiply the resources with which he has been entrusted. Michael loves Jesus and believes in the power of the local church to meet the needs of those it serves. With more than four decades as a pastor and church planter, Michael brings a hybrid blend of practical, situational experience together with the timeless truth of the Gospel message.

Which is why I am thrilled about XLR8. Comparing pastoral leadership and church building to Formula 1 racing in a brilliant way that only Michael could pull off, XLR8 takes you on a pulse-pounding joyride of discovery. Rather than focus on performance, Michael knows that the secret to successful F1 racing is momentum—which is true for pastors as well. While drivers must balance speed and control to gain and sustain momentum for their race, pastors must learn to adjust to God's pacing and timing while steering the church for growth and impact. Both racers need a dedicated team, a pit crew who share their faith-fueled vision for the long haul.

You don't have to be a racing fan, though, to receive the incredible benefit and blessing of Michael's inspiring message. Because he knows leadership is not about beating other churches in size or splash, in numbers and name recognition, in budgets or buildings—the race we're in is the one God has set before us. This is the race Paul references in Hebrews 12:1—the race we must run with perseverance even as it takes us off-road and into uncharted territory, following God's guidance, Christ's example, and the Spirit's leading.

I've been humbled and privileged to share what I know with Michael and see him make it his own for maximum impact in advancing the church. And I know firsthand how well Michael continues to run his race of faith, persevering for God's glory and the advancement of His church. He loves people and knows how to connect with almost everyone. Michael is always introducing people to other people, building relationships, and constructing bridges. The respect he earns does not come from admiration for his wit and winsome personality but from his dedicated faith, his servant's heart, and his commitment to the Kingdom.

You see Michael's loving heart and fierce devotion in his marriage to Valery, in how he talks about his adult children and beloved grandchildren. But clearly, for Michael, it's not simply about his passion and commitment to people. He understands leadership, its necessary systems, and what it takes to succeed no matter the setting, situation, or circumstances. His ability to make you laugh or enjoy his storytelling is unrivaled, but it's the way Michael uses them for greater purposes that linger on.

So buckle up, my friend. Roll down the windows and feel the wind in your face as you accelerate into a new season of learning what it means to run your race with more Spirit-fueled momentum. Learn from Michael how to drive in a way that remains true to your calling and the unique gifts, talents, and abilities God has given you. I promise this driver's manual will be one you review again and again, for insight and inspiration, for what you need to keep going—and what you need to keep you going—as you follow God and steer His church.

You are about to be exhilarated by XLR8!

—*Chris Hodges*
Pastor, Church of the Highlands

FORMULA 1

I love cars, but I have a checkered history with them. About the time I was having a mid-life crisis, my wife Valery and I bought a Volkswagen EOS, a small black convertible. We loved that car, especially during Sydney's gorgeous summers, cruising along the beautiful south beaches and through the National Park that borders our suburb. We put the roof back so we could feel the wind in our hair—Valery, me, and Charlie, our very spoilt Cavoodle—it was the dog we bought before you needed a second job to buy any dog ending in "-oodle." By this time, we had a couple of grandkids, and the backseat of the EOS was too small for car seats. What the grandkids want, the grandkids get. I went to the car dealership to check out mid-sized SUVs. The one that caught my eye was a Range Rover Evoke, which, believe it or not, is also a convertible. When I got in it, I realized it wasn't big enough, so the salesman showed me a full-size Range Rover. When he told me the price, I said, "I wanna buy a car, not a small country!"

He walked me over to another SUV—it was beautiful . . . and he could tell that's what I thought! "Take it out for a spin," he insisted.

I sensed myself swirling down into his "persuasive sales vortex," so I yelled at myself, *Pull out! Pull out!* I quickly came up with an excuse:

"Sorry mate, I just realized I need to pick up my wife at the mall." Phew, that was close.

He smiled and told me, "No problem. Pick her up in it, and keep it overnight."

As I signed the insurance paper for a test drive, I thought, *What am I doing? I thought I told him I couldn't take it for a drive.* As he handed me the key fob, he said, "Drive it like it's yours. Take it through the National Park! You'll see how much fun it is to drive it."

As I pulled out of the dealership, my perspective radically changed. I suddenly hoped I'd see every person I'd ever known (especially those who had recently left our church) so they'd be really impressed with me and my wheels. I drove to the mall with the moonroof open and the windows down. When I pulled up next to Valery on the sidewalk, I used my sleaziest voice: "Wanna lift, baby?" She got in ... and marveled that I was even thinking about this vehicle. I went back to my normal voice: "Hey, let's take 'er for a spin!" We headed for the entrance of the National Park. It was beautiful at dusk. I drove (a little above the posted speed limit) around sweeping bends under the canopy of ancient eucalyptus trees. It handled like a sports car!

When the last rays of the day were just seeping away, we headed back home. As we rounded a bend, a gray flash streaked in front of us. It was a kangaroo, and it had smashed the grill of the SUV! The roo went to its heavenly reward of the great green pasture in the sky ... I couldn't say the same about the vehicle.

The next morning, I had to take the car back to the dealership. For those who know me, you know that subtlety is not my strong suit! Rather than slinking in with my head down, I made my grand entrance. I loudly exclaimed, "Hey guys! Great to see you on this beautiful morning! I've got some good news and some bad news: The good news is that my wife and I absolutely love the car! We looove the car!!! The bad news is that it's not quite in the same state as you gave it to me yesterday."

We really did love the car, and now, I had my sights set on a black one just like it: black wheels, dark tinted windows ... 007 all the way. As I was mid-sentence, negotiating a price for it, the salesman ran into the room. He breathlessly told me, "I talked to the sales manager, and we want to offer you a deal ... on the car you just brought back." (Code for the one you just trashed!)

I wanted to say, "Yeah, but who wants to buy a wrecked car, even if I'm the one who wrecked it?" But before I said a word, he told me their offer was to waive the $2,000 deductible, discount the car another $8,000, and fix the grill good as new. I asked if they'd also put the fancy wheels on it, and they agreed. I signed on the spot. I called it my "kangaroo discount." It proved to be a great deal for everybody ... except, of course, the roo.

I'm using cars as a controlling metaphor for the message of this book, but not just any cars—those that race in Formula 1 competition. It's all about momentum. In F1 racing, momentum is the force generated by a car in motion, and it determines how fast a car can accelerate and maintain speed through the corners and down the straights. Several factors affect the momentum, including aerodynamics, tire wear and pressure, engine power, and the driver's skill. Drivers have to balance speed and control to build and maintain momentum throughout the race. When a car is trying to pass another, it must have adequate momentum in the split second of the passing opportunity.

It's all about momentum.

Some people may assume that racing is the easiest sport in the world . . . because we do what they do when we sit behind the wheel in traffic several times a day! But this is different, really different. F1 drivers are involved in rigorous physical training so they'll be at their best physically and mentally in the long, hard, amazingly fast grind of a long race. They practice and work with mechanics to fine-tune the car's performance. Before the race, they take practice laps and visualize every turn. A day or two later, the race begins! The noise and the speed would cause distractions (and wrecks) if they weren't prepared. It's one of the most thrilling sports in the world.

Come with me on the analogy here . . . Being a pastor is much like driving an F1 car. Leading a team and a church requires the creation, building, and maintaining of momentum. Many factors determine the church's speed of growth, but on the track, the driver is in control. He constantly monitors every gauge for speed and efficiency, and he makes adjustments based on input from his team, his pit crew. Together, they can run faster and longer.

F1 cars have eight forward gears, and this book has eight gears that will help you gain momentum and take every advantage of it to grow your church.

The Pit Crew is an integral part of the team. As for F1 Drivers, so too for you as a lead pastor. That's why the book is specifically designed for you and your team.

The eight chapters (or gears, as we'll call them) breakout neatly so that in two months teams can work through this together, reading each chapter individually and then discussing it as a team, with particular reference to answering the following questions:

- What does this mean for us as a team and as a church? (It's all in the application.)

- What are we already doing that's heading in the right direction? (Celebrate these!)
- What can we tweak that would really get us moving forward? (You may be closer than you think.)
- Are there any theological or philosophical emphases which should be discussed as far as discipleship is concerned? (Your theology outworks in your praxis.)

I've been in Christian leadership roles for forty years, and this book has been a decade in the making. During that time, I've invested more than 10,000 hours to provide insights and resources for 1,000 lead pastors and their teams. The book you hold in your hands is the product of these interactions. My goals for the book aren't small.

XLR8 is designed to help you:

- Demolish any frustration at being stuck as a leader and a church,
- Accelerate the fulfillment of the dream God has put in your heart,
- Fulfill your call by reaching far more people with the saving gospel of Christ and seeing your church grow radically,
- Mobilize forty percent of God's people to be active "bringers" every week,
- Engage every guest through a practical, effective pathway to become fully devoted followers of Christ and vital church contributors,
- Activate authentic discipleship for the majority of people in your church,
- Double your small groups and equip your group leaders to be the backbone of discipleship at your church,
- Restore health and strength to your volunteer teams, both in volume and life-giving culture,

- Develop a seamless leadership pipeline to deliver an "embarrassment of riches" for your current and future vision for church, marketplace, and missionary leaders,
- Release untapped financial resources by identifying and curating the gifts of generosity, and
- Steward a disciple-making movement of God's Spirit so His people are released into ministry and your church doubles its impact in your community.

Let me give you an idea of where we're going. This diagram illustrates the hub of the wheel and the eight gears:

One of the reasons I'm so committed to seeing churches XLR8 their impact is that I was the recipient—a most unlikely recipient—of a church's gospel-centered ministry. I had been sexually abused as a young boy (more on that in the Seventh Gear), and I ran as far away from God as I could go. I hoped alcohol, drugs, and sex would numb the pain and give me some sense of pleasure. They did, at least for a while, but at a staggering cost.

When I was younger, I'd gone to a Catholic church a few times. On Christmas Eve, when I was twenty-one, I drank all day at a pub. Long after the sun went down, I walked down the street to the Catholic church. They were having Midnight Mass, and I stumbled in and sat on the back row. During the service, I sensed a voice—not an audible voice, but a voice nonetheless—asking without a hint of condemnation, "What are you doing?"

I responded, "I'm in Ssszurch. Whad djjjou doing?"

Even in my drunken stupor, I knew what God was saying: "You know better than this. You know that I have something far better for you."

This was pretty close to a Damascus Road encounter with God, except that Paul wasn't drunk when he had his. And I kept drinking because it was the only way I knew to cope with life.

One night, I got behind the wheel of a vehicle heavily intoxicated. It didn't end well. I was driving way too fast between "watering holes," and I lost control of the car. It rolled and flipped onto its roof. All I can remember was hanging upside down in the car, suspended by the seat belt. I could have been killed that night. Instead, I had only a few scratches on my back. I lived to tell the story.

This near-death experience stirred my heart. I had come to the end of myself, so I went to the Catholic church again. When the priest said, "The Lord be with you," I shouted, "And with you!" Needless to say, I was the only one shouting. People looked at me like I was a lunatic, but I thought being loud might bring me closer to God.

One night I invited all my friends to come over to my parents' house for my twenty-first birthday. I started earlier in the afternoon with a stack of beers and some "gifts" a few of the fellas brought over to aid with the birthday cheer. But I didn't "cheer" for long. By 7:30, I was laid out on the sofa, dead to the world. Far from my finest hour. They partied all around me while I lay face down taking up three places to sit. When I woke up the next morning, the memory of the voice in the church haunted me. Something had to give.

A friend told me, "Hey, I went to a crazy church in the city. There are pretty girls there. Do you want to go tonight?" It was Christian Life Center Sydney... the precursor to what became one of Hillsong Church's campuses.

God and pretty girls... what's not to like about that? We went to church, and for the first time in my life, I heard and understood the gospel of grace. At the end, Pastor Brian Houston led us in a response. He told everyone to close their eyes, and those who wanted to trust in Jesus to raise their hands. I raised my hand. I hoped no one peeked to notice. Was I being upsold here, and was I the only goose in the room raising his hand? I was so self-conscious. Then he said, "Stand up." I stood up, but I was afraid I was the butt of a joke in front of all these people. Then he said, "Come forward." I wasn't sure I could do it, but then a very pretty blonde girl walked past me. I thought, *Hmmm. It can't be too weird if she's going forward*, so I got into the aisle and walked behind her. Pastor Brian prayed for us, and then a young man talked to me about my decision... and I never saw the pretty blonde again. When I left the church, I knew life was going to be different... but I wasn't sure *how* different.

The next morning, the guy from the church called to follow up with me about my decision to trust Jesus. I was living in a dive we called "Yobbo's (read Red Neck) Mansion," an eight-bedroom house in the celebrious suburb of Connells Point right on the river. At any time, between eight and a dozen young men lived there. To get to your room, you often had to step over and around empty pizza boxes and beer bottles. I was just getting out of the shower when one of my mates yelled, "Murphy, some guy from that church is on the phone for you!" He was the fellow who had counseled me after the altar call the night before. He was neither cool nor the kind of person I would have ever have hung out with.

Dripping wet with a towel around me, I picked up the phone. He was so cheerfull and said, "Michael, a group of the fellas are getting together for lunch at the university. Do you want to come?"

My mind was saying, *Are you kidding? No!* but I heard the words come out of my mouth, "Sure, buddy. I'll be there."

Lunch wasn't as awkward as I feared. In my mind, they were on the bottom end of cool, but they were really great guys. I met the head of all the University Fellowships in Sydney. He seemed like a sharp guy. Some time later, I got a call from Wayne. Immediately, before he explained why he was calling, I made the assumption that he was going to ask me to help him run the fellowships at all the universities in Sydney. Is it possible to be any more arrogant and any more clueless at the same time?

By the time I'd hit puberty, I'd never known a time when I didn't have a girlfriend—not because I was so handsome and dashing, but because I was so insecure that I desperately needed someone to validate me. A couple of weeks after I became a believer, my girlfriend, whom I'd previously been living with, also trusted Christ. The person who followed her up was a Qantas flight attendant named Valery Stokes. My girlfriend and I broke up, and my heart was taken with Valery. We fell madly in love and got married within six months. (At this point, I often explain that the Bible says, "It's better to marry than burn," and Valery was burning up! When I tell this part of the story, my beautiful wife of forty years this year gives me a sharp and well-deserved jab in the ribs.)

I was working as a rep for Pfizer Pharmaceuticals, and the church where I had found Jesus was in my area. Not knowing my place as a new believer, I rocked up fairly often to hang out at lunch with Brian and the other pastors. (Isn't that how it's supposed to work?) They were kind and gracious, but I'm sure my brashness and overconfidence were pretty obvious to them.

After Valery and I had been married for about twelve months, we moved out to join Brian and Bobbie Houston as they planted Hills Christian Life Center (which later became Hillsong Church). Not long into this journey, we were asked to lead a small group. Looking back on it, I can vouch for Valery's spiritual maturity, but mine? Hmmm, not so much. I had been reading the Bible since I'd gone forward, but I was such a novice in my understanding of the Scriptures. On Monday nights before our group meetings, I opened a *Strong's Concordance*, Matthew Henry's *Commentary*, and books by J. Sidlow Baxter. (I went for tonnage in my resources.) I fasted every Tuesday to prepare my heart to lead the group, and God worked. Our group multiplied five or six times over the couple of years. (I didn't know that was unusual.) Our growth caught the attention of the pastors at the church, and Ps Brian said he wanted to talk to me. I remember it like it was yesterday. He was dropping me off from a prayer meeting, and we were parked outside our dumpy little fibro house, and he turned off the car engine (that was unusual.) He said that if the church continued to grow like it was, then I was the kind of person that he would like to have on the team as a pastor. I wanted to shake his hand, look him in the eye, and say something spiritual like, "Praise God, Pastor, that would be awesome!" Instead, I burst into fits of tears (ugly tears) like a volcano had been uncapped inside of me. And so the adventure continued! My role on staff was to help build a robust pastoral care system which would help care for the growing numbers of people. In a few years, the church grew to over 5,000 people. We were on a bronco. It was a wild ride!

Though I thought I'd never leave Hillsong, my heart started to stir whilst on a trip to the U.S. with the family. We were driving along the backcountry of Arizona near Sedona, and Deuteronomy 1:6-7 came to mind and spoke directly into my heart: "You've been at the mountain for long enough, turn and take your journey... to the South by the seacoast."

It was time to broach the subject with Valery. I told her what I thought God may have been saying, and she simply replied, "Well, we had best pray about it then!"

We were currently serving at Hillsong, in the Hills District of Sydney, when I heard about a church that needed a pastor in an area near my old stomping ground in the South near the seacoast.

One thing led to another, and we eventually became the pastors of this forty-year-old church in the Shire. I made a mess of it in the first two years. Everything that worked so well at Hillsong fell flat at ShireLive, which is now called Horizon. I had a ministry of blessed subtraction, and God used this difficult season to moisten the clay of my soul to reshape me from the inside out. I had a lot to learn.

God gave me a passion for discipleship, and in the next few years, we grew to 330 small groups. Valery was my secret weapon. The church had four struggling women's groups when we started, and in two-and-a-half years, she grew that ministry to over 125 women's groups.

Later, I started the Christian Men's Network, and soon, 300 churches were using Ed Cole's videos for men every month. It was phenomenal content. I devoured it for myself, and I gladly recommended it to churches across New South Wales. I also became the chairman of Youth Alive NSW (New South Wales), a powerful movement of God among young people. I got involved with our denomination in church planting and church growth.

In 2013, we launched Leaderscape to use everything I'd learned in decades of resourcing churches so we could champion lead pastors. We have two main goals: First, to get churches unstuck. Lifeway, an American research organization, reports that sixty percent of churches have plateaued or are declining, and more than half saw fewer than ten people become Christians in the year before the study was concluded.[1] That was before Covid, and we all know the impact of the lockdowns on church involvement. A more recent Barna survey found that forty-two percent of pastors have considered quitting because the stress of leadership has brought them to the brink of burnout.[2] Our second primary goal is to accelerate the growth of churches. We can't make it happen, but we can catalyze the momentum generated by the Holy Spirit through church leaders.

The three "pillars" of our efforts are an extensive curriculum to be used onsite and online; our "Founders Collective" of weekly zoom calls to our partners to provide patterns, processes, and presence; and one-to-one coaching for pastors. Some pastors look down on church growth strategies because they claim, "It's not spiritual." To me, there is no dichotomy separating strategy and spiritual power—they go hand in hand. For instance, Moses meticulously described the plans for the tabernacle (in seven chapters in Exodus), the oldest management structure is found in Exodus 18, David received intricate plans from the Spirit of God (1 Chronicles 28:12), the Spirit gave Paul a very clear plan to travel and plant churches, and the plan of salvation is clearly spelled out in the Gospels and the letters.

---

[1] "How Many US Churches Are Actually Growing?" Aaron Earls, Lifeway, March 6, 2019, https://research.lifeway.com/2019/03/06/how-many-us-churches-are-actually-growing/

[2] "Pastors Share Top Reasons They've Considered Quitting Ministry in the Past Year," Barna, April 27, 2022, https://www.barna.com/research/pastors-quitting-ministry/

When I hear people say, "We just need a revival," I wonder if at least some of them want God to do it all so they can sit back and watch. Yes, we need a revival, but we need Spirit-filled men and women to listen to God, plan and pray, and work hard to see the harvest. So, is it the Spirit, or is it our efforts? Paul answered that question in his letter to the Philippians. After his powerful poem about the deity, sacrifice, and exaltation of Christ, he tells them, "Therefore, my dear friends, as you have always obeyed—not only in my presence, but now much more in my absence—continue to work out your salvation with fear and trembling, for it is God who works in you to will and to act in order to fulfill his good purpose" (Philippians 2:12-13 NIV). We work, hand in hand, with God as He works. Both, not one or the other.

God has given me the unspeakable privilege of coming alongside pastors and their teams to impart principles and help them apply them in their communities. These concepts have proven to be fruitful in churches large and small. I'm amazed that God would use me in this way, but that's the way of grace, isn't it?

Are you ready? You're the driver of your F1 car, I'm the mechanic, and your team is the pit crew. The Spirit of God is your fuel. Hold on tight. It's going to be a great ride!

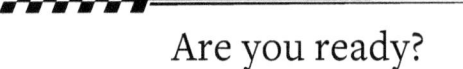

Are you ready?

START YOUR ENGINES

Formula 1 drivers know that a lot rides on them being at peak performance when they start their engines on race day. They take nothing for granted. Their regular workout regimes include strength training, cardio and flexibility exercises, and endurance training. Nutritionists carefully plan the drivers' diets. They need fitness and stamina to have razor-sharp reflexes and stay alert when the car produces high G-forces in sharp turns and blazing straightaways. They spend time in racing simulators to become intimately familiar with the layout of the racetrack, and they anticipate every turn, deceleration, and acceleration on the course. Drivers work closely with engineers and mechanics to analyze data from earlier races and practice runs. Their goal is to shave every shred of time off every lap. The driver and the entire team engage in rigorous and detailed planning to discuss opponents' usual strategies, tire management, fuel consumption, and every other aspect of the upcoming race. Before and perhaps after the practice laps, the driver walks the track to observe any anomalies or features not noticed before. Every corner is, to some degree, unique, and the driver must know exactly what to expect. Throughout this preparation, drivers use mental exercises to stimulate focus and minimize anxiety. Then, they start their cars, pull into their starting positions, and are ready for the green flag.[3]

Each F1 driver is responsible to get the most out of the team's efforts and the tens of millions of dollars invested by the sponsors. A pastor's responsibility is much greater. We represent the King of Glory, and our "win" is advancing His kingdom. Just as an F1 driver goes through rigorous preparation before he puts his car in line for the start of a race, pastors must be ready to lead. The single most important element in being ready is prevailing prayer, bathing our hearts in the presence and the power of God. Prayer isn't a method to manipulate God to fulfill our agenda; it crafts our hearts so our deepest desire is to fulfill His agenda. I'm not aware of any great movement of the Spirit throughout church history that wasn't founded on the bedrock of prevailing prayer.

Four strengths come from this kind of prayer:

1) SPIRITUAL PURPOSE

On a mountain in Galilee after the resurrection, Jesus gave His followers marching orders. We know it as "The Great Commission." In Matthew's Gospel, this was given as His last word, His clear directions, His unmistakable purpose. What was it? To make disciples ... not those who raise their hands or come to the altar, not just people who will come and sit in our services, not people who are baptized and we never see them again, and not necessarily people who volunteer or are on our teams. These people may or may not be genuine disciples! A disciple is one who follows Jesus—it's that simple and that challenging. It means we have His heart for people, we treat them with His love and truth, we have no partiality toward race or financial status or

---

[3] See "8 Things F1 Drivers Typically Do to Prepare for a Race," Gaming How, May 10, 2023, https://www.gaminghow.com/blog/8-things-f1-drivers-typically-do-to-prepare-for-a-race

beauty or intelligence, and we use all our resources for God's glory. We love everyone because Jesus loves one who deserved nothing but condemnation: me . . . and you. Disciples make an impact in the way Jesus made an impact, by loving the unlovable and accepting the misfits and outcasts. And He loved them enough to enlist them in the greatest enterprise the world has ever known: reaching every person on the planet with the gospel of grace and building multiplying disciples who will reach more and multiply more.

Look at your church's purpose statement. Does it reflect the purpose of making multiplying disciples? If not, get out a pen and paper and start over.

2) SUPERNATURAL PRESENCE

This isn't some odd, mystical thing. It's having a relationship with the God who sent His Son to die the death we should have died so He could give us the honor Jesus deserves. Theology should always lead to more than a full mind; it should point us to the very heart of God and open our hearts to experience the wonder of His pardon, presence, and power. I don't think I'm unusual in that I need reminders of my new status as God's beloved child. It's too easy for old, negative, condemning, doubting voices to drown out the gentle whisper of God, so I need to regularly feast on the truths of who I am "in Christ." You'll find a full list later in the book, but let me offer a taste of them here:

- I am a child of the Most High God, thoroughly loved by Him and accepted in the Beloved.
- I am a called and anointed minister of the Good News of the Lord Jesus Christ and His kingdom, and I'm committed to walking worthy of this high and holy calling.
- I choose "amazing" every morning. I bounce out of bed first thing knowing that the day has huge opportunities in store for

me. I am excited and confident each morning as I launch into the day.
- I am free from the feeling that I am not enough or that I am letting God or others down—the cross and His grace really are enough.

My guess is that you would probably benefit from starting each day with similar truths dominating your thoughts. God created us to live in His presence. We shouldn't allow any hurt we've suffered, trial we are going through, sin we have committed, blessing we have received, or economic level we have attained in life make us neglect, hide from, or get bored with God's presence. Even when we've sinned, God is waiting with open arms to receive us into His presence (Luke 15: 20-22). Just as a fish can't survive outside water and needs to be in water to thrive, we can't survive these challenging and uncertain times outside of God's presence. The more time we spend in His presence, the more we'll thrive and shine.

> Even when we've sinned, God is waiting with open arms to receive us into His presence.

3) STRATEGIC PLANS

A clear vision needs an adequate vehicle: the bigger the vision, the bigger the vehicle. Executing a good plan is the way you create and increase the size of your systems to accomplish your God-given purpose.

When our kids were still relatively young, and consistent with our family priority of "making memories" at all costs, we decided to embark on a four-week fly-drive trip across several states of the USA. We landed in LAX, then boarded a flight to Las Vegas to stay at the newly opened MGM Grand—the hotel with a theme park inside the hotel! (Whaaat!)

Following two days of bleary-eyed jet-lag mental fog, it was time to pick up the vehicle that would take us to see the Grand Canyon. We'd booked a medium-sized vehicle, thinking that would be enough to take us to our destination. (Cue fits of hysterical laughter!) Two upgrades later, we drove out in an eight-seater van which was able to fit all of our children and the dozen or so bags that accompanied us.

Yup, the size of vehicle has got to be large enough to fit the full extent of the vision, in our case, to transport all of us and our bags to our destination.

Throughout the 90's, with the birth of the church growth movement, there was a strong emphasis on the importance of leaders having a clearly defined vision. I was all in . . . I believe wholeheartedly in vision. But a vision can be fragile. As I write, post-pandemic, there is a fresh hunger for a greater move of the Spirit of God. I jest with pastors that "the Holy Spirit is finally making a comeback!" So this is totally a wonderful thing. Right? I'd give it a hearty "maybe."

Obviously, our broken, hurting world needs a fresh move of the Spirit of God, a Third Great Awakening. The church herself needs renewal and restoration to get back in line with God's purpose. So, what's the problem? Why the hesitation? And what's with the "maybe"?

I have a conviction that amidst the increasing craziness of our generation, people want to hit the reset button. If that's the case, the church is perfectly positioned to capture this moment . . . but we must know where we're headed. What are the directions?

I have this "thing" about me that I can't head off on a journey without having a good handle on where I'm headed. Though I have a reasonable sense of direction, who needs it these days with GPS? Still, it's not unusual for me to sit in the driveway until I have it all locked and loaded and I know exactly where we're headed and how we'll get there. Then, we're off!

Who knows how our family ever negotiated our way around the United States with those old-school paper maps? Truth be told, we barely did. You see, my beautiful wife is smart, prophetic, a gifted communicator and discipler, and she worships her heart out with pitch-perfect voice, but it would be fair to say that directions are not her strong suit. And Valery was the navigator.

If your destination is absolutely vital, so too is your road map, and the turns you take can make or break you.

I've spoken to a lot of pastors over the past decade. Thousands actually. Most pastors start out their ministries at least with a passion to see something significant happen for God's kingdom. Fueled by their personal version of a "burning bush encounter," they're called by God to bring transformation to their town and lead throngs of people to a life-changing encounter with the love and power of Jesus.

Most pastors can identify their destination, but fewer know how to get there. College and seminary have taught them how to preach and teach, how to pray, and how to pastor people—all admirable and needed skills to shepherd their flocks. But most pastors are less equipped to craft the necessary plans they need to reach their God-given vision, and these plans are absolutely necessary for the creation of processes and practices to see it actually come to pass.

Now, I know that when I speak this way, some leaders tune me out. They believe planning is unspiritual, lifted straight from some college's business course textbook. I honestly get that, but this analysis is at least partially off-target. Throughout the Bible, we see leaders plan— and execute their plans—but always led by the Spirit of God.

Some leaders avoid planning because they don't feel comfortable and competent in this area. Their fallback position is insisting that God will do it all, which sounds very godly and spiritual, but eventually leads to stagnation and confusion. Sometimes it's easier to expect God to do it all than to take up our part of God's discipleship plan.

Jesus absolutely did say that He would build His church; however, He never promised to make one disciple! That's our job under the leading of His amazing Holy Spirit and under the authority of His Word. Though I understand what pastors mean when they cry out for God to do more, but from heaven's perspective, God may be saying, "I'll give you more when you use what I've already given you. I've already sent my Son to die the most heinous death on that Roman cross, He rose again with the keys to hell and the grave, I sent the Holy Spirit not just to be with you but to be in you, I have given you the authority of the name that is above every other name, and I canonized My Word for you. With all this, I asked you to pray for laborers to go out into the harvest and to go make disciples. So let's go!"

Yes, we must pray. Yes, we must listen. Yes, we must trust God to do what only He can do, but we need to be careful to avoid spiritualized abdication from our responsibility to win people and build disciples. There is no dichotomy between the call to pray and the challenge to obey and lead. They are like the tires on both sides of an F1 car. We need good tires on both sides if we're going to race well.

I'm not whistling in the wind. Not infrequently, I hear a dangerous dichotomy between the Spirit and strategy and systems: presence and power . . . and plans and processes. I've even heard some say, "We want more of God. We don't need all those strategies," as if these things were mutually exclusive.

God created the world, and for a season, He enjoyed perfect, intimate friendship with Adam and Eve until their choices wrecked that.

Since then, God has longed to be with His children. During the times of the patriarchs, He used selected mouthpieces who spoke on His behalf, and then only from time to time. This one-way monologue was hardly a replacement for walking with His kids in the cool of the day in the utopia of the Garden of Eden. Then He spoke to Moses and asked him to build a place where He could dwell in proximity to His children, the people of Israel. To get the plans, Moses had to venture up the mountain of God into the raging smoke, lightning, and thunder. Wow! This sounds like the epicenter of the Presence of God, and yet God gave him intricately written designs for every aspect of the tabernacle, even down to the furniture and objects used in worship (see Exodus 24-25). The pattern of presence and plans is repeated again and again as God related to His people, and it's still His pattern today.

As we make Christ's last command our first priority, we must seek His presence and trust Him for good plans. A friend recently told me, "Attention to detail is an expression of love."

4) SEAMLESS PROCESS

Good plans lead to effective praxis. Leaders create a culture, and the best leaders create a culture that brings out the very best in each person. Communication, delegation, and feedback are essential, and again, all bathed in prayer to tap into God's limitless resources of love, forgiveness, and power. Much of the rest of this book is about this process, so there's no need to go into details here.

By the time the Formula 1 driver starts his engine moments before a race, he and his crew have worked hard to make sure their car, their strategy, and their communication are exactly right, but they've also studied their opponents and planned the race to compete against every strength and take advantage of every weakness in them. We have an adversary who has been around this track many times, and he's crafty. Peter gave leaders a warning and a promise:

> *Be alert and of sober mind. Your enemy the devil prowls around like a roaring lion looking for someone to devour. Resist him, standing firm in the faith, because you know that the family of believers throughout the world is undergoing the same kind of sufferings. And the God of all grace, who called you to his eternal glory in Christ, after you have suffered a little while, will himself restore you and make you strong, firm and steadfast. To him be the power for ever and ever. Amen.* —1 Peter 5:8-11, NIV

Be alert, be strong, and stay on the track when the storms roll in . . . and they will. The center of the Momentum Map describes what's necessary for pastors and their teams to get to the starting line ready to go!

As I previously indicated, the concepts in this book are most helpful if the pastor uses it with his team, and perhaps, with his board. The shared insights, creativity, and interactions will inspire, challenge, and instruct as they pursue God's best together.

PIT STOP: OWN YOUR MORNING

F1 drivers know the importance of getting off to a good start in every race. In the same way, we need to get off to good starts every day. Some of us wreck our days by hitting the snooze button, and when we finally wake up, we feel behind all day. And many of us dive straight into emails and social media . . . which is letting other people determine how we start our day. We need God's truth and His promises to become the default mode of our minds and hearts. How can that happen? By imprinting them every morning. Let me share my morning formula. Of course, feel free to modify it as you wish, but this is what works for me.

> We need God's truth and His promises to become the default mode of our minds and hearts.

MORNING SCHEDULE

1) I wake up at the same time every "push" day (5:15-5:30 a.m.). This makes me consistent in what I do and how I feel.
2) I start every day going over this routine:
   - » EXERCISE   30 mins
   - » WORSHIP   15 mins
   - » BIBLE   30 mins
   - » PRAYER   15 mins
   - » FORMULA   15 mins
   - » DAILY GOALS   15 mins

   (From there, I read the Scriptures, or I get into work if studying is slotted for later.)

   I spend then thirty minutes, four days a week exercising.
3) I spend at least 1/2 hour every single day working on ME. Reading a book, watching a training video, working on my goals, journaling, meditating, etcetera. This time is scheduled and blocked off. All my devices are turned off so I'm not interrupted.
4) I work from a list, and every day before I leave work, I map out my priority list for the next day.
5) Every week I list down the following in my journal:
   - » Top three to five most valuable activities for the week
   - » Learning lessons and corrections
   - » Study list (what do I want to learn next week?)
   - » Gratitude

6) Every month I list the following in my journal:
    » Top seven to ten most valuable activities for the month
    » Top learning lessons and corrections
    » Planning and reflection for the next forty days
    » Gratitude (who do I need to tell I'm grateful for them?)

I take a sabbath every week to be still, to chill, and to recalibrate.

7) I prioritize my family, connecting at least every two days with our kids, grandkids, and my mum, no matter where in the world our schedule takes us.
8) I protect a solid one month for vacation every year.

I take a special break every quarter with Valery for three to four days somewhere around the globe as we travel helping leaders.

I remain very focused, enthusiastic, and passionate about achieving Leaderscape's goals.

CONDENSED DAILY CONFESSIONS
IDENTITY
1) I am a child of the Most High God, thoroughly loved by Him and accepted in the Beloved.
2) I am a called and anointed minister of the Good News of the Lord Jesus Christ and His kingdom, and I'm committed to walking worthy of this high and holy calling.

MINISTRY
1) I am one of the leading momentum catalysts for church pastors and leaders in the world, helping senior church leaders to "get unstuck" every time.

OPPORTUNITY

1) I choose "amazing" every morning. I bounce out of bed first thing knowing that the day has huge opportunities in store for me. I am excited and confident each morning as I launch into the day.
2) I anticipate and execute each morning my full-person workout for my spirit, soul, and body.

FREEDOM

1) I am free from the feeling that I am not enough or that I am letting God or others down —the cross and His grace really are enough.
2) I am free from the fear of rejection or failure. I act without fear of either and feel confident, strong-minded, and energized.

BLESSING

1) I know my value, I honor my worth, I am worthy in Christ of His abundance, and I feel grateful and at ease with what Jesus continues to provide me. I understand that the essence and purpose of God's blessing and prosperity are to help others more vulnerable with a hand up that points to God's love for them.

CONSULTING

1) I am an excellent leadership consultant. I feel powerful, confident, and assured in my skills to reach out and attract new lead pastors that we can help.
2) God's Spirit gives me strategic and creative wisdom as I help others tackle their challenges and in doing so, help lead pastors improve their lives and churches.

3) I always give more than what I am remunerated for, all of my clients are happy, and they spread the good word about how we have helped.

HEALTH AND FITNESS

1) I look after my body as the temple of the Holy Spirit so it is healthy and disease-free, specifically avoiding carbs and sugar and eating stacks of greens and drinking adequate amounts of water.
2) I maintain a fitness and strength regime which consists of, at a minimum, thirty minutes per day (five days per week) spread between cardio and weight-bearing exercises.
3) I am intentional about actively stimulating my own mental health and sharpness, including keeping my stress at manageable levels by constantly unburdening my soul to the Holy Spirit.
4) I make regular investments in my marriage to ensure that after forty years, we are not merely surviving but thriving.

ACTION AND MOTIVATION

1) I am a self-starter who does not need any external force to motivate me. All of my motivation comes from within and from Jesus, and I can call on it at will. This makes me feel unstoppable and powerful.
2) Each and every call I make or appointment I have, I start with a high level of positive expectation and prosperity. I know that right now, somewhere, a lead pastor's life is better, more fruitful, and more prosperous because of my resources and services.
3) I love taking action. I feel courageous and exhilarated by taking action, and I build extreme momentum and prosperity when taking action.

PERSONAL DEVELOPMENT

1) I am focused and committed to increasing my personal and leadership capacity through my time with God and key mentors, as well as what I read and resource myself with.
2) My positive affirmations, goal-setting, and strategic action make me a highly successful leadership consultant. I feel positive and grateful for the favor and blessing that flows to me through the grace of God.
3) I then look at some of my favorite passages about the presence and the glory of God, for instance:

> *You will show me the path of life;*
> *In Your presence is fullness of joy;*
> *At Your right hand are pleasures forevermore.*
> —Psalms 16:11

Presence is a big deal to God!

Throughout all of history we read the story about God searching for us, born out of His desire to be with us . . . to establish His presence with us.

IN THE GARDEN

- Adam and Eve were in the Garden in God's beautiful presence, but they rebelled and they lost the presence of God.
- We see Him coming to them after the fall.
- It would be unusual for Him to do this for the first time then.
- It's reasonable to assume it was His habit.
- Patriarchs and Prophets
- Genesis 12
- God got the plan back on track by giving Abram (Abraham) promises that His blessing and presence would be restored and he would be a blessing to generations and all nations.

- Exodus 19
- Moses on Mt. Sinai
- God's presence comes down.
- It freaked the people out.

THE FATHER

"Behold what manner of love the Father has bestowed on us, that we should be called children of God! Therefore the world does not know us, because it did not know Him. Beloved, now we are children of God; and it has not yet been revealed what we shall be, but we know that when He is revealed, we shall be like Him, for we shall see Him as He is. And everyone who has this hope in Him purifies himself, just as He is pure" (1 John 3:1-3).

JESUS

"Behold, the virgin shall be with child, and bear a Son, and they shall call His name Immanuel," which is translated, "God with us" (Matthew 1:23).

THE HOLY SPIRIT

"And I will pray the Father, and He will give you another Helper, that He may abide with you forever—the Spirit of truth, whom the world cannot receive, because it neither sees Him nor knows Him; but you know Him, for He dwells with you and will be in you" (John 14:16-17).

And then I write in my journal. This is one day's entry:

Though now it's mid-morning here in Huntington Beach (middle of the night back in Sydney), it's still dark in our room thanks to some block-out curtains.

I feel strangely drawn through the song "Show Me Your Glory" to a ten-year-old-school album by "Jesus Culture, Live in New York with Martin Smith" . . . and that's where I continued something that has been brewing for a few months now . . . a fresh pining and hunger for the presence of Jesus.

It's very unusual for me to add even just a few songs from any album to my worship playlist, but to add eight out of sixteen doesn't happen. Now I admit that this may be just "my thing" right now and may not translate to you, but I wanted to share it with you just in case.

I am right now sensing a fresh desire in my heart to experience His presence more than ever. Let me go back to several months ago when a young pastor friend spoke of his renewed focus on experiencing the presence of God every day. What should have been a routine conversation then "move on" became a conversation that gripped my heart.

Then a few months later another friend shared in a podcast I was filming with him how without the presence of God, he had nothing . . . again, as it tends to happen when God is trying to get through to me, his words stuck deeply in my heart.

Then a mini video "popped up" (God is the master of popups) in my daily devotions on the Exodus on the presence of Go: https://www.youtube.com/watch?v=b0GhR-2kPKI

Now this morning, as the tears flowed, I experienced the next moments of what I had been sensing. I sat with His presence washing over me for over two hours as song after song brought beautiful waves of His Holy Spirit flowing over my heart.

Though songs like "Pursuit," "Walk with Me," "Song of Solomon," "Show Me Your Glory," and "Did You Feel the Mountains Tremble" all deeply moved me, the song "Holy Spirit" put into words the cry and prayer of my heart right now.

I'm not sure where this is leading me, but I have a quiet sense of excitement and anticipation to see what He wants to do in me and a strong confidence that it's only good.

Like I said, maybe this is just for me right now...but just in case it's something more, I am prepared to risk a few "good for yous"...

Here's a link, but don't just listen... really lean in: https://music.apple.com/au/album/live-from-new-york/1440851330

Pastor, staff member, and church leader, you don't need to follow my example to the letter but tailor the first moments of every day so your heart can bask in God's presence, love, and glory. It'll make a difference. I guarantee it.

FIX YOUR NETS

Virtually every pastor on the planet has heard the warning to "close the back door" because too many people attend a few times and are never seen again. After thousands of hours of consulting with pastors over the past two decades, I've come to the conclusion that the real problem isn't "the back door"—it's the front door.

If you focus your attention on the front door, there won't be nearly as much of a problem with people leaving out the back. The task of pastors and their teams is to create an impeccable, gracious, welcoming experience for guests so that trust is built quickly. You will make friends, and, coincidentally, more individuals and families will consider your church their spiritual home. They'll be more willing—indeed, eager—to commit to the next steps of discipleship.

As the XLR8 Track shows, you can only fulfill the Spiritual Purpose of your church if you attract guests, build trust quickly, and take them to your Growth Track where they can feel welcome. Then they can take the next step of involvement . . . and the next.

"Now may the God of patience and comfort grant you to be like-minded toward one another, according to Christ Jesus, that you may with one mind and one mouth glorify the God and Father of our Lord Jesus Christ. Therefore receive one another, just as Christ also received us, to the glory of God"

—Romans 15:5 -7

FIRST GEAR: ENGAGE EVERY GUEST

Entry points can be thrilling . . . and dangerous. When I was just a lad of four, our family lived in an apartment above a funeral parlor at WN Bulls in King Street Newtown—long before it became a cool, hipster, inner-city suburb. My dad was the funeral director. For me, living in the "concrete jungle" of the inner city felt cramped. To add some spark to my little life, I loved racing down the sloping concrete backyard on my vehicle of choice, a cool little three-wheel scooter. (I wasn't into Formula 1 yet.) As the firstborn of my mum and dad, I played by myself, so to make it more interesting, I "played chicken" with the big back gate. One day, the gate won! I slammed into it with such force that my chin split open and blood spilt like a firehose! I ran into the house and yelled for my mum. She took one look at me and knew she had to take me to Camperdown Hospital for stitches. The problem was that the only vehicle available was a hearse. I was really young, but I knew what a hearse was for. When I got in, I wondered if the cut on my chin was far more serious than my mum let on! We arrived at the hospital—I was still alive. And after some necessary needlework, Dad drove us home—still kicking. This was my first interesting, if worrying, experience with motor vehicles.

Some people who walk through the doors of our churches for the first time are relaxed and eager to participate. (You can put that number of people in the hearse my Dad drove.) Most people arrive with more than a little apprehension, even if a friend or relative has invited them. As we'll see when we look at small groups, the first questions people ask aren't, "What does the Apostle John mean by 'propitiation' in his first letter?" No, they're asking, "Do I like these people?" And even more important, "Do they like me?" If we look at our front doors through that lens, we might be surprised by the way our churches make the first connection with guests.

If you only make an announcement during the service to welcome guests and ask them to fill out a card, some will but many won't, and the information on the card will be spotty. A judicious, excellent, focused, warm welcome to roll out the red carpet for "new friends" of the church—guests or visitors—makes an indelible impression and begins a heart-to-heart engagement leading, hopefully, to genuine discipleship.

I can't tell you how many pastors have told me, "Michael, we have lots of visitors every week, but it's really hard to get their information so we can follow up with them."

With all the grace I can muster, I say, "I hear that a lot, Pastor, but your statement tells me there's a lot more that can be done to connect with visitors. Let me show you how." I then explain the heart and the process I'll outline in this chapter, and I can report that those who implement it don't have this problem any longer . . . and the results in guest retention and involvement is nothing less than astounding.

Most churches have parking lot attendants and greeters at the door, but I'm talking about more . . . much more. A superficial and transactional welcome, a warm smile, and clear directions are the usual goal, but in my estimation, that level of initial connection misses a colossal opportunity. I recommend pastors select very carefully for their VIP Team. I sometimes call them "Undercover Angels" or "Navy SEAL Connectors," which raises the team's vision of their crucial role. These people don't wear church-branded t-shirts. Yes, they wear shirts, but normal, everyday clothes so it doesn't look to the guests that they're being treated like commodities. This team is separate from greeters, though they need to work in tandem. They may or may not stand near the front doors, but their antennae are on high alert as they look for people who may be there for the first time.

We offer a script that can be modified for each church (found at the end of this chapter). Members of the VIP team walk up to the person or family and introduce themselves and ask how long they've been coming. They ask how they found the church and affirm the friend who brought them, the post on social media, or whatever it was that prompted them to come. If it's a parent or a couple with kids, the VIP team member can say, "Where would you like your kids to go this morning? They can sit with you, or we have a wonderful kids' program. Would you like me to introduce you to the leaders in their classes? I have to tell you, they're fantastic!"

On the way to the kids' classes, the team member can give just a one-minute story of getting involved in the church. After warm, affirming introductions to the kids' teachers or childcare volunteers, it's important to assure parents (many of them anyway) that they haven't just left their kids in the hands of ax murderers. The point is that some parents feel very uneasy about leaving their kids with strangers, so the team member needs to provide assurance. On the way back, the team member can ask if they'd like some good coffee (and be sure it's really good coffee!). Then, he can say, "Are you connecting with your friend who invited you?" If the answer is "yes," help them find the friend. If the answer is "no," he can tell them, "My wife (or husband) and I would love for you to sit with us. Would that be okay?" If this answer is "yes," take them into the auditorium, introduce them to your spouse, and continue to build rapport.

By the time the service is over, a friendship has probably budded. The team member can offer, "Hey, I'd like to give you a call this week to see how you're doing and answer any questions you might want to ask. Would that be okay?" If the guest gives his or her number, it's ethically right to then say, "Our pastor loves to connect with guests at the church. Would you mind if I give him your number so he can send you a text to let you know how glad he is that you came today?" If the person is hesitant, that's fine, don't push it. Subsequent visits to the church will offer opportunities to get this information into the church's database.

The spirit of this conversation is "no pressure—all warmth." The VIP team member can say, "The reason I want to call you is that I want you to find a church that's just right for you (and your family). This one may be a good fit. If not, I'll be glad to give you some suggestions of other churches in the area. And if you want to go to the Growth Track meeting next week to find out more about our church, I'll be glad to go with you." (More on Growth Track later.) This is a laid-back approach, which is actually more attractive because it's openhanded and openhearted, with no pressure or any hint of manipulation.

To go the second mile, I encourage VIP team members to invite the person, the couple, or the family out to lunch after the service. This supercharges trust, and it may shock the guests, especially if you pay for it. I was in northern England sharing this concept of a VIP team, and the people at the church were really into it . . . until I mentioned taking guests to lunch. The mood of the room suddenly collapsed, so I asked, "What did I just step in?"

One of the men said, "Michael, we show up an hour early, tidy things up, and pray, and we stay for the entire time. Now, with this lunch invitation, you're asking us to act like . . ." He paused for a few seconds as the wheels turned in his mind, and then he smiled and said, "Like Christians."

Everyone laughed. I said, "Yes, that's exactly what I'm asking you to do. Being a loving, kind Christian is much more than serving in a role for a few hours."

A good parallel is the concierge at a fine hotel, like the Ritz Carlton, or the most elegant stores, like Nieman Marcus, or the maître d' at most exquisite restaurants. For our anniversary many years ago, Valery and I made reservations at a restaurant called Senses in Amsterdam. It was a Monday night, so the choices were a bit limited, and we'd never been there before. When the Uber dropped us off, we weren't at all impressed with what the restaurant looked like on the outside. We looked at each other, and with a resolve in our steps, we decided to brave the unknown—maybe feeling a little like someone who attends a church for the first time or the first time in a long time. The entrance was very ordinary indeed, but the moment we stepped through the door, ordinary was no more. The maître d' greeted us, we were escorted to a table set beautifully, and the meal was incredible. At one point, the chef came out of the kitchen to be sure we liked what he had created for us. Yes, we liked it. In fact, it wasn't just the food; the entire experience went far beyond our expectations. It was like we'd been invited into a large, loving family of the most caring people and were served the most delicious food. As you can tell, it was quite memorable. We still talk about it, and we can't wait to go back—and here I am telling you about it two decades later. That's a real-life parable about the potential of a church's VIP team. What if that was the experience of every person who walks through the doors of our churches?

When people give their details on a card or online, it's more than information; it's an expression of trust. If they don't trust much, they won't give much information. If a genuine relationship has begun and trust is developing, they'll feel free to offer more information about themselves.

In my opinion, the people recruited for the VIP team need to be the most carefully vetted, chosen, and trained in the church. Yes, that's what I said because that's what I believe. It won't do to have a few warm bodies opening the door. We can go far beyond that, but only if we have a vision for making guests who walk in the "front door" feel like a million bucks. Yes, people are busy. Yes, as a pastor, you've got a lot on your plate. But this crucial interface with guests is often the make-or-break moment in their comfort level, their willingness to come back, and their commitment to take steps to become true disciples. This first expression of love can make all the difference.

Imagine Jesus himself turning up at your church one Sunday morning wearing a t-shirt and jeans, and he brings a couple, Bob and Jan, and their two kids to church for the first time. He hands the four of them over to someone in the lobby and says, "I brought Bob and Jan today. Would you please look after them for me?" Actually, I don't think we need to imagine this scene. We only need to open the eyes of our hearts to see more clearly. I believe that every person who comes to your church is brought by Jesus, and He hands them over to someone at your door or in your lobby. They are indeed God's guests. The Spirit of God has already been working in them to make them hungry for the Word and thirsty for the presence of God. They got into a conversation about God at the coffee shop, they overheard someone mention your church at a football match, or they experienced the kindness of a neighbor who attends your church. It happens in a million different ways, but it happens! God is wooing them and handing them to you and your people. Your job is to be sure guests are as loved and welcomed as if Jesus was giving you their hands ... because that's exactly what's happening. That means they're not just newcomers or visitors; they're guests of the King.

In the closing chapters of his letter to the Romans, Paul told them to put their experience of grace into compassionate action: "Now may the God of patience and comfort grant you to be like-minded toward one another, according to Christ Jesus, that you may with one mind and one mouth glorify the God and Father of our Lord Jesus Christ. Therefore receive one another, just as Christ also received us, to the glory of God" (Romans 15:5-7). Other translations use the word "accept" or "welcome" instead of "receive." The point is that Jesus went way out of His way (to say the least) to reach out to welcome and receive you and me. If our hearts are melted by the warmth of His love, we'll do all we can to welcome and receive those He loves who come to our churches.

From the parking lot to the lobby to the children's classes to the auditorium, every step needs to be "an awkward-free zone." I've been welcomed by people who look like they've been in front of a computer their entire existence. They barely made eye contact, and I felt like it was up to me to make them feel wanted. Yes, there's a place for everyone in the body of Christ, but not everyone is the right fit for every role. Using deodorant and having most of their teeth isn't the full list of criteria for those who first connect with guests. When pastors become intentional about choosing the right people for the VIP team, they'll find that these recruits have a huge heart for people, exude authenticity, and see their roles as critical in the process of building multiplying disciples. With that heart and that vision, they'll be very easy to train and launch. Most pastors view their worship team as absolutely essential because it's the face of the church, but the worship team isn't the "first face" of the church. The VIP team can be. This team is even more important than the worship team.

> This welcome team may even more important than the worship team.

However, when guests arrive at our front door, we can blow it in any number of ways. For instance:

- Nobody greets them or makes eye contact.
- Too many people greet them, and it's weird.
- A greeter wants to hug every person, which is fine for a few, but for others...
- Someone thrusts a card in their hands to ask for their information, and that's the greeting.
- The welcome is insincere.
- The guests don't know where to go next, and no one is there to tell them.
- The greeting is handled from the stage in announcements instead of personally.
- The pastor oversells the benefits of involvement, which may impress a few but turns others off.
- Not having a VIP team, not having the right people on the team, and not having enough of them.
- No deodorant and missing teeth. Enough said.

A carefully vetted and selected team will roll out the red carpet and give concierge service to guests. One of my mentors, Dr. Ed Cole, used to say, "You can't mold dry clay." We "prepare the clay" of guests by giving them an experience far better than they expected. Then, after the service, when the team member invites the guest to attend a growth track—and attend with him—enough trust has been built so the person is far more likely to say, "Sure. I'd like to go with you." The offer to go with them is infinitely more compelling than, "Hey, you ought to try out our Growth Track. It starts next week."

Let me get on my hobby horse about an issue related to all this: announcements. Years ago, the government in America had a campaign, "Say No to Drugs." I'd update and modify it for pastors: "Say No to Announcements"—not all of them, but most of them. I've been in services when it seemed that the announcements lasted longer than the sermon. The people needed a recorder or paper and pen to keep track of them all. I recommend no more than four or five; the rest can be put in a handout. The few that make the cut need to align with the mission. Typically, they would include:

1) Welcome guests—people who are new or haven't been for a long time—and point them in an attractive, organic way to fill out the cards or give their information online. "We're so glad you're here. We want to make your experience truly wonderful for you and your family. As you take a good look at us and decide if this might be the best church home for you, it would help us if we have a little information about you. That will help us help you get connected." If they've been warmly welcomed by someone on the VIP team, resistance will be minimized.

2) Talk about the benefits of the Growth Track (more on this soon), and give the details of the next series.

3) Explain the importance and benefits of getting involved in small groups. To make this more seamless, many pastors are weaving this into their messages to be sure people understand

involvement in small communities of believers is the hothouse of spiritual growth. If you talk about the impact of groups in the sermon, and especially if you share a story about a miracle or breakthrough in a group, you might need only give an announcement about how to sign up to join a group.

4) Explain that giving is an opportunity to expand the Kingdom of God. Many people give online today, but most churches still offer some method of giving at or after the service.

That's four. If there's a church-wide event coming up, you can add it as the fifth, but that should be the limit of announcements. It's not the time to announce the next men's ministry series, women's ministry event, youth camp, craft workshop, or any of dozens of other things going on. Everyone you add beyond the four or five dilutes all of them. A few are essential; many are not. I was in a church not long ago when I counted ten announcements. I may have missed one or two, but I counted ten. To save time, the person ran through them like they were being shot from a machine gun. The effect? Boredom and confusion. That's not the impact you want to have on anyone, especially those who are new to the church.

Beyond the number of announcements, I suggest you consider "imparting vision" in your announcements. This means that each one needs to be carefully crafted to connect people with the heart of God and the mission of the church. When we aren't thoughtful and targeted with announcements, they may do more harm than good. Similarly, in the absence of strategic thinking, we often try to fill the void with too many words and too much emotion.

Covid was very difficult for churches, and many still haven't fully recovered from the lockdowns. One of the insights we gained from that difficult season came from countless reports: to the chagrin of many pastors, the people didn't miss the sermons all that much because they could watch them online, but they certainly missed the sense of community by being apart. The VIP team is the first and most important connection point to begin building community.

When I begin consulting with pastors and their churches, most of them are getting about one percent or less of attenders to make the initial contact on a card or online. With vision, training, and execution, they increase that number to three, four, or even five percent. It changes the game. At first, when I ask pastors about their percentages of responses, they often respond with a quizzical look and say, "I'm not sure. Nancy, one of our office assistants, handles that."

Depending on my relationship with the pastor, I might say, "Pastor, you don't need to know everything, but you *really need to know* this number. It's important."

We can identify several streams of information about guests and those who have been attending only a few weeks. Some fill out a physical guest card, some use a QR code on the back of the seats or on the screen, some have registered when they check their children in at kids' church, some showed up for the Growth Track series or a small group, and some become first-time givers. Churches need a system to consolidate all of these streams into a powerful, flowing river of information used to follow up with newcomers.

Les and Angela Harvey are the lead pastors at Church of the Pines in Tyler, Texas. As is commonly the case with churches we work with, their response rate for visitors making a connection and giving information was about one percent of the 300 people attending. The Harveys became very intentional about recruiting and training a VIP team, and within eighteen months, their response rate was five percent of their new attendance of 750, close to forty each week. (300 to 750–I know of no pastors who wouldn't be thrilled with that!) So how did they grow so much so fast? Because guests felt warmly welcomed, started a relationship of trust, got involved in all aspects of church life, and brought their friends. It's not magic; it's just kindness in action.

Bishop Jonathan Woods is the pastor of All Nations Church in Fairfield, Alabama. His services are something to behold. There is so much excitement, such a terrific response from the people, a fabulous choir and band, and amazing preaching. For Bishop Woods and his team, the Sunday service was the epicenter of their impact. As we talked about connecting more effectively with guests, he caught the vision. When I met him, he was receiving less than one percent response from guests in giving their contact information. They were averaging about 400 each Sunday. Within eighteen months, about 3.3 percent of guests were responding and giving their details, and the congregation had blossomed to 1,100.

Chris and Jan Beard are lead pastors at Peoples Church in Cincinnati, Ohio. He wrote *Remarkable*, which has become a trusted resource to help pastors move their churches to be more inclusive and multicultural. The church had a guest response rate of half of one percent when I met the Beards, and in fifteen months, it grew to two percent. During that time, the church grew from 300 to 500 and an additional 150 to 250 online. Chris told me, "During this time, the Peoples Church Network grew from six churches to ten, now reaching about 2,000 people. All of our churches are learning and applying the Leaderscape principles and processes."

Anthony Cox is the pastor of the City Campus of River Valley Church outside Minneapolis, Minnesota. The church is just down the street from the intersection where George Floyd was killed by police on May 25, 2020. The church stepped into the chaos and anger in the community to offer comfort and the promise of ultimate justice through Christ. Like the other examples I've mentioned, City Campus was receiving about a one percent response when I met Anthony, and in twelve months, that number had grown to 3.5 percent. The impact was similar: the church grew from 600 to 800, with a few peaks to 1,000, over that time.

I could use many other churches as examples of those who have seen dramatic results in their growth just from this one strategic change. (If that's enough for you and you want to run with it, you can quit reading now. But I have many other ideas I want to share with you!)

XLR8's promise is that if you'll select, recruit, train, and empower an outstanding VIP team, you'll make far better connections with your guests, build trust, funnel more of them into *Growth Track, and grow your church.*

Before the driver takes his Formula 1 car up to the starting line, he and everyone on the team—from the owner to the guys who sweep up after work each day—look carefully at every aspect of the track, the car, and the competition to be sure they get off to a fast start. Don't make any assumptions about the guests whose presence can jumpstart your church's growth.

> Don't make any assumptions about the guests whose presence can jumpstart your church's growth.

PIT STOP: SENSORY WALKTHROUGH

One of the exercises I recommend for pastors and their teams is to put themselves in the shoes of a guest and walk through the process. Most of us are so focused on what happens during the service that we seldom even think about the interactions at the door and in the lobby. People assimilate information through their five senses, so I ask the pastor and the team to observe what they see, smell, feel, taste, and touch. But there's another dimension: spiritual intuition. Guests come back to church primarily because they felt and sensed something positive, not because they encountered brilliant theological exposition. (The two aren't mutually exclusive, but we can't teach profound theology if people aren't in the seats.) I encourage staff teams to walk through the entire experience with a guest-centric lens. Most of them have seldom or never walked through the front door when anyone was there. They come early and often through a different door. This exercise usually opens their eyes to see things they've never thought about before . . . or ignored because they didn't think it was very important . . . and it wasn't on their job description anyway.

- Is the sign easy to read? Are directions to the front door clear?
- Who are the attendants in the parking lot? Are they smiling or all business? (A few churches have implemented a system so that when a parking lot attendant identifies a guest, he calls someone on the VIP team in the lobby to meet them at the door. Wonderful! That's treating people as God's guests.)
- What do they see in the lobby? What's the atmosphere? Is the coffee area obvious? Is the coffee aroma wafting in the lobby?
- How many VIP team members are there? Where are they stationed? Are there any means of making connections other than not recognizing them?
- How do parents find the kids' rooms? Who is greeting them at those doors? Have they been selected and trained to serve as VIPs?
- When guests walk into the auditorium, what's the environment? Temperature? Lighting? Ambient music?

Don't take all this for granted. Do the rudimentary work of putting yourself in a guest's place on a Sunday morning, and pay attention. Then, create a dynamite VIP team, limit your announcements, and follow up with your new contacts.

SCRIPT FOR VIP TEAM MEMBERS

First, raise your antennae to watch and listen for cues. For instance: How comfortable does the person feel? Do parents seem really concerned about their kids going into the nursery or kids' church?

You have only a second or two to make a good first impression, so smile, empathize, and affirm. Use or adapt these statements and questions, and each time, listen well so you'll know how to follow up with the right response.

"Hi, I'm Michael."

"Have you been coming for a while?"

"How did you find us?"

"What brought you here today?"

"What's your coffee of choice? Latte, cappuccino, black, with cream?

"Allow me to introduce you to someone on our amazing kids' team."

"Would you like to sit with my wife and me (husband and me, friends and me)?"

"Wanna grab coffee (or brunch or lunch) after the service?"

"Would you mind giving me your number so I can give you a call sometime this week?"

"Are you okay with me giving your details to my pastor? He loves to send our new guests an email to thank people for coming."

"Then had the churches rest throughout all Judaea and Galilee and Samaria, and were edified; and walking in the fear of the Lord, and in the comfort of the Holy Ghost, were multiplied."

—Acts 9:31

SECOND GEAR: EXPLODE YOUR GROWTH TRACK

The first car that I actually owned was purchased from a second-hand dealer along the notorious "Auto Alley" on Parramatta Road in Sydney's Western suburbs. I should have been warned off when I saw that out the front of the Car Yard was a car proudly being displayed up a tree! That's right, the car was suspended in a tree! What better way to welcome unsuspecting, cash-strapped prospective car buyers as they entered the shady car yard! In other words, people like me.

The salesman must have "seen me coming" as he slipped me into an early 70's white Ford Cortina. He promised it was in great shape, and to seal the deal, he gave me a super easy finance rate. (Months later, I realized I'd probably paid double what that thing was worth.)

What was I thinking? Still, it was a car . . . and now it was my car. As if the repayments weren't burning a big enough hole in my pocket, after only owning it for a couple of months, I looked outside one afternoon to see smoke pouring from the engine!! My car was on fire! Literally on fire! It was an inauspicious beginning to my career of car ownership. I really needed to make better decisions about getting from point A to point B . . . as in the physical so too in the spiritual—which is what Growth Track is all about.

Growth Track is an introductory group for those who are new to the church or new to the faith (or both). Many churches have a three- or four-week series beginning on the first Sunday of every month. Whatever term is used in different churches, most pastors realize the need to have some kind of environment where people's questions are addressed, and they can feel known and loved, at least to some degree. When I ask pastors if they have a Growth Track, almost inevitably, they say, "Yes, we certainly do. We've had one for years."

But when I ask, "How well is it accomplishing the goal of integrating these people into the life of the church by planting them in small groups?" they hang their heads and mutter one of several standard evasive answers, such as "Okay, I guess," "I hope so," or "I really don't know."

I've observed a couple of common problems:

First, the vision and goal of Growth Track isn't widely shared, so few people in the church actually bring people into this class. In other words, the universe of those inviting guests is far too small. Second, the class itself is often too content-heavy. The leader or a video about the church takes up most of the time, leaving precious little opportunity for people to get to know each other and for questions to be asked and answered. An overload of content compromises the quality of connection.

Some time ago, I was consulting with a bi-vocational pastor whose church had about 350 in attendance each week. I painted a picture of what Growth Track could be: highly engaging, some humor, some vulnerability by the leader, and so much warmth that people walk out of the room each time saying, "Man, wasn't that wonderful! I love the way the couple leading it reached out to know us and welcome us. And we learned a lot about the church, too. This is the church for us!"

When I finished painting this picture, the pastor lowered his head. I asked, "What's up, buddy?"

"I've been blowing it," he confided. "I've packed our Growth Track with content—so much that I have to rush or go too long each week. I thought imparting information was the goal. Creating a warm environment? That's a revelation to me."

I asked, "What do you do in your life and ministry that's really meaningful to you?"

His eyes lit up, "I lead a men's group, and I absolutely love it! We meet for eight weeks in the fall and eight weeks in the spring."

"How does it work?"

He was really into it now. "The first week, I ask my wife to speak to the men."

I jumped in, "Wow! That's really interesting," I said (but actually thought, 'How odd!' After all it's a men's group!) What does she say?"

"She tells the story of the time early in our marriage when she wrote me a seven-page letter detailing everything that was wrong with me!"

"I'm sure the guys love that!" I remarked.

"And then we both share how God has been so good to us. Our marriage hasn't just survived; it has thrived. We love each other more today than ever—and we like each other most days, too."

I told him, "Dude, that's your opening story in your Growth Track!"

He looked like I'd hit him in the face with a wet fish. "Really?"

"Yes, really. Vulnerability is the currency of engagement. When you're vulnerable, people lean in to listen and know more. Your openness tells them more about grace, forgiveness, and love—and what your church is about—than any exposition of doctrine or a dozen handouts about church programs. The people listening think, Wow!

If they went through that and came out better and stronger, maybe there's hope for us and our marriage.

Vulnerability is the currency of engagement.

It's crucial to pick the right person to lead a Growth Track: It's not Terry the Teacher or Dennis the Demon deliverer. It's Colin the Congenial, the one who puts people at ease and connects quickly and well with all kinds of people. One of the best I've ever seen is our daughter Elyse. She became the leader of the Growth Track for Oasis Church in downtown Los Angeles, which is in Koreatown. Founded by Philip and Holly Wagner, and now led by Julian Lowe, it is one of the most diverse congregations in America: about twenty-five percent African-Americans, twenty-five percent Latinos, twenty-five percent Caucasian, and twenty-five percent Asians and a few others—a true melting pot and an image of what the new heavens and new earth will look like. Elyse is the quintessential Caucasian girl: blonde hair and freckle-faced. Before she began leading it, their Growth Track averaged about forty people each series. She created such a loving, welcoming atmosphere that their average grew to between 250 and 300. The size was already beyond the size of even a large small group, and as it grew, Elyse needed to find ways for people to connect with each other. She had people sit in small group circles, and each circle had two leaders. But before people walked through the door of Growth Track, there was a crucial factor: in fact, the single ingredient that led to the incredible increase was to tell every small group leader and VIP team member to take guests to Growth Track or at least meet them at the door for the first meeting.

What prompted this strategy? One weekend, Elyse was invited to a party, but she was tired and decided not to go because she didn't know many people (or anyone) there. But her friend Melissa told her, "Come with me. I'll meet you at the door, and we'll go together." At that point, her decision to go or not go wasn't just about the party; it was much more about her friendship with Melissa. Elyse's connection with her friend was more important than her discomfort about going to the party.

Elyse connected the dots with Growth Track, and when she asked every church leader to bring visitors to the meeting, or at least meet them at the door when they arrive, the attendance rate increased almost immediately by fifty percent... and the numbers kept rising as leaders saw the results of their gracious invitations.

As always, follow-up is essential. The leaders of Growth Track (or the leaders of the circles) call those who attended and say, "Thank you for sharing this week. It meant a lot to everyone in the group." And if the person didn't show up one week, the leader can say, without a shred of condemnation or manipulation, "We missed you last time. I want to bring you up to speed on what we talked about so you won't feel out of step next week. I want you to meet a couple of people who are new to the group. I'll meet you at the door and introduce you to them next week."

It's essential to take the extra step for leaders to invite and bring guests to Growth Track, and it's just as important for the Growth Track leaders to follow up each week with brief phone calls. So here's the point: the weekly Growth Track meetings aren't the main thing... the main thing is the relationships built before, during, and after the meetings.

For years, churches have designed classes to connect with new believers or those who are new to the church. Before the earth's crust hardened, we used to have ten-week series for new believers to ground them in the faith. Today, people rarely commit to anything new that's over three or four weeks. The Church of the Highlands in Birmingham, Alabama, has one of the most effective strategies. Their Growth Track has three steps, each covered in a single meeting: the first about membership, the second about personality and spiritual gifts, and the third to help people find a team where they can serve most joyfully and effectively. Other churches call their classes Next Steps, Connect/Encounter, Welcome Home, or something else. It doesn't matter what you call it, but it matters a lot how it's constructed—and even more, it matters how well it accomplishes the goal. The goal? Many pastors assume the goal is disseminating information about the church. Wrong! The goal is to inspire people to get involved in a small group or a service team, or both. Information is just one piece of the pie.

I don't want to get too far ahead of myself, but let me say something about the goal and the strategy: Discipleship is much more than people attending on Sunday mornings. It involves heart-to-heart interactions. It can certainly happen in a mentoring, one-on-one relationship, but scale requires the use of small groups to stimulate people to follow Jesus wherever He leads them, to be whatever He calls them to be, and to do whatever He calls them to do. For this to happen, pastors need to recruit, equip, inspire, and place outstanding (not just good enough) group leaders, excellent curriculum, and an outstanding process to funnel people into groups. We'll address the training of group leaders in the next chapter. This one is about the funneling process. To be clear: groups aren't the goal; they're the vehicle to accomplish the goal of discipleship.

I've seen many churches use the three-meeting model. Let me break it down a bit:

- Week one is a warm welcome and an explanation of "this is us." Give people a picture of what's important to the pastor and the leaders of the church so they can make an informed decision about whether the church is a good fit or not. It can include:
- Begin with refreshments and introductions, with one icebreaker question, such as "What do you like to do in your spare time?" "What was your first car?" or "What was your favorite vacation?": ten to twelve minutes. (Remember, they're intuitively asking the questions, "Do I like these people?" and "Do they like me?" The answers are crucial!)
- Share your vulnerable story, maybe with some humor: five minutes.
- Outline the story of the church, its history, and values, including Jesus, the cross, the resurrection, the Scriptures, families, kids, missions, etc.: seven minutes.
- Anticipate questions people may or may not be willing to verbalize, such as the pastor's salary being set by an independent board, security of children, perhaps a doctrinal statement, and other issues that are germane to newcomers. Don't get into long explanations. Your statements need to be long enough to be informative but short enough that people don't get bored. Tell people to go to the church's website for more information: five to eight minutes.
- Give time for questions and answers: five to ten minutes.
- Introduce next week's topic: "Next time we're going to unpack some observations about the incredible potential of each person, including you and me. It will be so encouraging. You don't want to miss it."

- Give them links to a personality inventory and a spiritual gifts questionnaire, and ask them to fill those out before next week.
- End before the allotted time is up.

The content should be no more than twenty-five to thirty minutes. The rest is interaction and QandA.

Elyse has two rules for the circles: Everyone needs to meet a friend, and everyone needs to say something. This is communicated early in the meeting so everyone has realistic expectations.

- Week two is about each person discovering their God-given personality and spiritual gifts, with an eye toward making an impact for the Kingdom of God. Many churches use brief personality instruments and a spiritual gifts questionnaire. The point isn't to have everyone with their heads down all the time; it's to give them insight into how God has wired them so they can fulfill their divine purpose.
- Begin with refreshments and introductions. Ask people to tell a little more about themselves, perhaps where they grew up, how they met their spouse, or their favorite sports team. Give each one a soft time limit of two minutes. The limit is necessary because there's always someone who seizes the opportunity to tell his or her life's saga: ten to twelve minutes.
- Explain how insights about your personality and spiritual gifts have benefitted you, and inject some humor if appropriate. Ask those who have completed their homework to share what they discovered. Don't shame those who haven't. Tell them that's just fine, and remind them to complete them: twenty-five minutes.
- Introduce the topic for the third week by saying, "Next week, we'll wrap up our three times together, but as you'll see, your impact is just starting. We'll look at a wide range of ways you can engage with the mission of the church, and we'll help you

find just the right place where you can use your talents for the glory of God."
- End before the allotted time is up.
- Week three points to continued involvement after Growth Track ends. Have several group leaders there, especially those who want to add people to their groups or are starting new groups. Serving teams are more transactional than groups, but team leaders can move the needle toward a group environment by meeting together for fifteen or twenty minutes before they start serving for a short Bible study, sharing, and prayer. Come to Week 3 with information and enthusiasm. You're about to hand the people in the class over to other leaders in the church.
- Begin with refreshments and introductions. This time, ask, "What was affirming or surprising about your personality inventory and spiritual gifts questionnaire?": ten to twelve minutes.
- Give a general explanation of the role of small groups and serving teams at the church, and lean hard into small group participation. Introduce the group leaders who are attending, and let each one share a minute or two about their group. Allow time for QandA. Total: fifteen minutes.
- Share an organizational chart or a list of opportunities to serve on a team. Answer any questions people might have: ten minutes.
- Give people a paper so they can sign up for a group or a team. Make sure they give their contact information: three or four minutes.
- Thank everyone for being there, and share your enthusiasm for their role in God's forever family. Pray that God will bless them and their families and that He will use them in enormous ways to expand His kingdom: two or three minutes.
- End before the allotted time is up.

When I talk about this way of hosting Growth Track, many pastors ask, "What about new believers? And what about people who are seeking?"

Great questions. Thanks for asking. I recommend having one of your very best group leaders (or perhaps a board member or staff member) host an eight-week small group that covers the basics of the faith in a warm, encouraging environment where no questions are out of line. Alpha has a wonderful curriculum many churches use. (Go to Alpha.org for more information.)

It's easy to assume just having Growth Track will accomplish the purpose, but it doesn't. The mistakes pastors can make when they launch Growth Track include:

- A vision of just having a Growth Track, not to see tangible, measurable results of future involvement.
- Too much content; not enough warmth, humor, vulnerability, and interaction.
- Failure to provide time for interaction.
- Having the wrong person leading it.
- Muddy and confusing messaging.
- Announcing Growth Track from the stage instead of people taking them there.
- Too little connection between the weeks of the Growth Track series because those who want to come on Week two or three have already missed part of it.
- Hosting it in a sterile, cold environment. (This can be a problem for mobile churches, but it's not insurmountable. Even a classroom or teachers' lounge can be warmed up with some ambiance.)

- Refreshments that send the wrong message, either too bare, like a box of donuts and bad coffee, or too extravagant, like Eggs Benedict and gourmet coffee.
- Not matching the size of the group with the size of the room. If you expect a handful of people when you start, put them in a small room where they don't feel like BBs in a stadium.
- The goals aren't clear.

In the First Gear, I suggested the pastor and the team do a walk-through and use their five senses to know what a guest feels when they come for the first time. In the same way, Growth Track leaders need to be sensitive to what those who attend see, smell, hear, taste, and touch. Here, like so many other places, Marshall McLuhan was right: "The medium is the message."

Sometimes I ask, "Pastor Jerry, how's your Growth Track going?"

He gets excited. "Terrific, Michael! We got a new coffee maker like you suggested. We have some music playing as they walk in, and we tune the lights to be more like a living room. People love it!"

"That's wonderful!" I intone. "What I'm really asking is: Did your Growth Track do what it's designed to do, getting people into small groups?"

I hope to hear Pastor Jerry tell me, "Oh yes, we had seven people join groups after the last one!"

"Terrific!" I told him. "Let's do a little more analysis."

Pastor Jerry had implemented the strategy to "Engage Every Guest," and his contacts grew from one to three percent of 400 attenders in just over a year: from four at first to twelve now. Twelve times fifty-two... that's over 600 in a year. The goal is to have forty percent of those go through Growth Track: that would be 240 people, which is an average of twenty each month, more or less, depending on holidays and summers. The next goal is to have eighty percent of the people who complete Growth Track join small groups; that's just under 200 people.

Look at it this way:

Lead Metrics	Guest Cards wk	Guest Cards yr	Growth Track	Small Groups	Back Door	Net Growth	%
Sunday 400			40%	80%	<10%>		
1%	4	200	80	64	-40	24	6%
3%	12	600	240	200	-40	160	40%

For a hypothetical church averaging 400 each week:
- Beginning: one percent response to the ask for cards of 400 people—four/week, 200/year.
- Goal: Forty percent of those who fill out guest cards go to Growth Track: that's eighty per year or a little more than six/month.
- Actual: Ten percent go to Growth Track: less than two/month.
- Goal: Eighty percent of them join small groups.
- Actual: A few join when their friends invite them, but there's not an effective system to funnel people into groups.
- In a year: four percent response: sixteen/week, sixty-four/month, with an effective Growth Track.
- Goal: Forty percent of those who fill out guest cards go to Growth Track: about twenty-five/month.
- Actual: If the VIP team and the rest of the church catches the vision, twenty-five/month.
- Goal: Forty percent of them join small groups.

- Actual: Ten people join groups every month out of Growth Track.

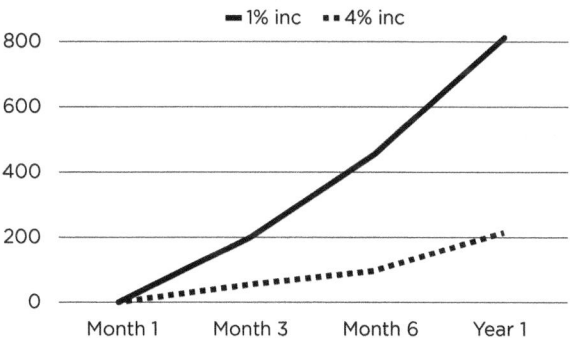

As you see, most pastors begin with a ten percent connection between guest cards and Growth Track, but Pastor Jerry was ahead of the curve. Before he had a VIP team, Pastor Jerry's system was doing better than that: twenty percent, or half of the goal, and half of those people actually joined a small group. Is that important? Vitally important. Small groups are the backbone of discipleship in the church. If they're strong, men and women, boys and girls, will become people who love Jesus, are filled with the Spirit, and live with the purpose of expanding the Kingdom of God. If small groups aren't given enough attention, and especially if leaders aren't equipped, they become just another nice program of the church, nothing more.

This perspective gives teeth to Growth Tracks. Environment is important, content is important, humor and vulnerability are important, and interaction is important, but the bottom line is the number of people who are handed off to small group leaders at the end of the last session. Discipleship is the purpose, and the very first step is getting people into small groups. This is *the* goal of every Growth Track.

A few pastors have told me, "Michael, we tried having Growth Track on the first three Sundays of every month, but we only had four or five people, and it was awkward. Now we have it every two months."

I asked, "For whom was it awkward? For you, maybe, but not for the people who come." If I had one, two, or three people, I'd communicate, 'Hey, I'm thrilled that you're here today! Grab a cup of coffee and a bagel, and let's get to know each other." I'd launch into the flow just like I would if there were thirty people in the room. Gifted group leaders know that more people aren't always good for the group's interactions. A more intimate group invites a deeper level of participation. Now, if you have fifty people, don't have people sit in rows like it's a lecture. Follow the lead of my daughter Elyse and have circles with skilled group leaders for each group of ten or so.

To be honest, when a pastor tells me he schedules Growth Track every other month, I cheekily ask, "So, I guess you tell your people not to invite anyone during the months you don't have Growth Track, right? After all, if they bring someone, there's nowhere they can send them to connect more fully with the church." They get the point.

Champ Callahan was the worship leader for his father, Ed Callahan, the lead pastor of Encounter Christ Church in Arnold, Missouri. But when Champ caught the vision of creating a cohesive flow to channel people into groups to be multiplying disciples, he asked his dad if he could leave his role in worship and become an associate pastor to lead this charge. He told me, "My time is better spent dialing in our VIP team and Growth Track to engage more people." He's doing a marvelous job. The church has grown so much that they've had to add services, and they still have space problems.

If you look at my recommendations in the first two gears and say, "Huh, there's not much discipleship so far," you're exactly right. The first two gears outline the seamless process that's meticulously curated to lead people into discipleship.

Another parable: A gardener with a hose wants to water his garden, and he has a big garden! He hooks his hose to the tap (faucet for my American friends–don't say I'm not trying to be culturally relevant now!) and turns it on full blast, but only a trickle of water comes out. It doesn't take a Ph.D. in horticulture to realize there's either a kink or a hole in the hose. He starts by examining the nozzle to see if it's working properly. If it is, he works his way back up the hose toward the tap to find the problem . . . and he doesn't wonder if there is one. When he finds the kink, he straightens it out, or if he finds a hole, he duct tapes it so it doesn't leak any longer.

XLR8's promise is that by making a few adjustments to your Growth Track strategy—in the VIP team bringing people, having the right people lead it, focusing on relationships more than content, and closing the deal with group leaders coming at the end to invite people to join their groups—you'll see a marked increase in the number of people in groups in your church. As I've said, this is where intentional discipleship really happens in the church.

In the same way, a twisted fuel line or one with a hole in it fails to deliver all the power a Formula 1 driver needs to be at his best. How's your hose, your fuel line? Is your system doing a great job of connecting with newcomers, building trust, and bringing them into Growth Track so they can be funneled into small groups to become multiplying disciples? That's what the first two gears are all about.

PIT STOP

If you're not getting the outcome of multiplying disciples you expected or hoped for, it's time to examine the hose, from the nozzle to the tap:

The culture:
- Do you have a culture of disciple-making? Do people understand their purpose is to deepen and expand God's kingdom? That's at the nozzle.
- What percentage of your people are in small groups?
- Are small groups effectively led, and are the leaders welcoming new people and multiplying?

The effectiveness of Growth Track:
- Are people coming out of Growth Track and joining small groups? What's the percentage of those attending Growth Track who join groups?
- Is Growth Track warm, inspiring, and informative? Is it led well? What is the ambiance?
- Are your people trained to bring people to Growth Track, not just tell them about it?
- Is your Growth Track scheduled for the first three weeks of every month?

Guest cards:
- How well are you drawing the streams of contact information into a single river?
- What is your percentage of guest cards in relation to attendance? Is that good enough?
- How well is the VIP team developing the early stages of trust with guests?
- What's happening at the front door? How well is your VIP team welcoming guests?

FILL YOUR FUNNEL

P astors and their teams have an incredible opportunity every Sunday morning (or whenever they hold their corporate worship services) to move the hearts, minds, souls, hands, feet, and wallets of everyone who attends. The problem is that they've been doing it so long that the elements have become second nature . . . so they don't analyze them unless something goes horribly wrong! In the next two chapters, we'll look at ways to maximize the impact of these services, and we'll explore a strategy to enlarge the number of people who attend.

We want to do far more than just have well-crafted services. We trust the Holy Spirit to work in and through us so that each person experiences the *Supernatural Presence* of God.

"For the word of God is living and powerful, and sharper than any two-edged sword, piercing even to the division of soul and spirit, and of joints and marrow, and is a discerner of the thoughts and intents of the heart. And there is no creature hidden from His sight, but all things are naked and open to the eyes of Him to whom we must give account"

—Hebrews 4:12-13

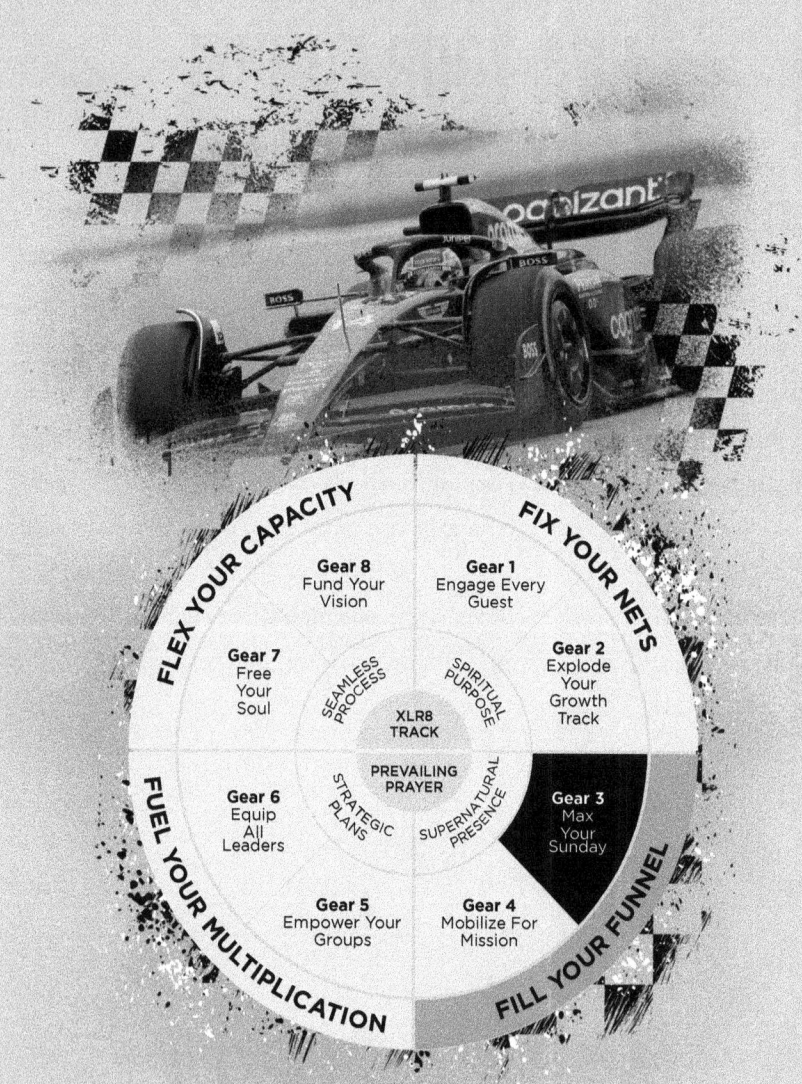

THIRD GEAR: MAX YOUR SUNDAY

I was in an executive meeting at our church when I received that call that no parent wants to get: "Your son has had a car accident on the freeway." Ryan had been driving his mother's almost new Toyota Corolla down to university in Wollongong (funny name, huh?), about forty-five minutes from our home. It was raining, and he was driving down a windy bend and lost it. The tires locked up, the car aquaplaned, slid sideways, and slammed against the barrier separating his side of the road from the oncoming traffic. When I pulled up, with my heart in my mouth, I realized that Ryan was fine . . . and the car looked totally okay as well. But a closer inspection would have revealed—and soon did reveal to the insurance agent—that the chassis was totally bent out of shape by the impact. The car was a total loss.

The panels and the paintwork looked unscathed, but the structure underneath was crooked. To the untrained eye, everything about the car looked perfectly fine, but it had huge hidden problems. Church services can be a bit like this. At first glance, they seem to be a well-oiled machine that's running fine, but underneath, there can be some big trouble.

Yes, I know that many pastors are experimenting with their schedule of worship services, and they're finding ways to connect with people at different times over the weekend and during the week to accommodate their busy lives. But since we have a long history of worshipping on Sunday, the first day of the week, I'm using "Sunday" in the chapter title. If you find this a bit constraining, I'm sure you'll give me a bit of grace.

By "Max Your Sunday," I don't mean you need to compete with Elevation Church, Church of the Highlands, or Lakewood. It's taking advantage of every resource you have with the purpose of honoring God and having the greatest impact on guests and your regular attenders.

Many worship services are church-centric, not guest-centric. In other words, we view what happens on Sunday mornings through eyes that no longer see clearly—we see only what we expect to see, what we've seen over and over and over again. Over time, we develop blind spots, but our guests take it all in. One of the best ways to take the blinders off is to invite someone to come to church and have your guest sit in the front row with you until you get up to speak. As your heart is sensitized to be in touch with what that person is experiencing, you may cringe at some things you've taken for granted for years.

It's important to identify your target audience. A leader told me the center of the target for his church is thirty-five-year-old men: "If you attract and keep them, they'll bring their wives, their children, and their friends." The strategy has been very successful. He said, "When you walk into our building on Sunday, you see a wide range of ages, but there's a disproportionate number of young families. The sermon illustrations are tilted toward young men, and programs are tailored to attract them and speak to the issues they're facing."

It's important to identify your target audience ... go from Church centric to guest centric.

Some pastors would object and insist, "We want to reach everyone, not just one segment of the community." I'm sure those who have a target audience would agree. They're certainly not saying they aren't reaching the wider community, but their emphasis on young men brings a large measure of excitement and fills the leadership pipeline with men and women in their formative years. From anecdotal information, I'd say that only about three out of ten pastors have identified a target audience. The rest need to at least consider it.

As we've seen, people experience life, including what happens on Sunday mornings, through their senses, including their spiritual senses. We've already addressed the importance of a walkthrough from the parking lot into the auditorium and the necessity of having the very best VIP team to connect with guests, but let me make a few additional comments about the first impressions before people walk into the auditorium:

- Station one: online presence. Is your website up to date with the latest technology? Is it easy to navigate? Some churches construct their content so that at least fifty percent of its content is geared to visitors, forty percent to regular attenders, and ten percent to leaders.
- Station two: outside. Does the building look nice? Does it need a facelift, or at least a fresh coat of paint? Is the landscaping something to be proud of, or does it look unkept and unloved?

Do people say, "Wow!" when they see the architecture and landscaping?
- Station three: the front doors and lobby. Do you have your very best people on the VIP team? We need to remember how unsettling—and even frightening—it is to walk into a church for the first time or for the first time in a long time. (For most of us, that happened when Napoleon captured most of Europe!)
- Station four: the children's area. Years ago, the selection of leadership teams focused on the pastor, worship leader, and youth pastor; finding someone to be in charge of the children's ministry was little more than an afterthought. Those days are gone. Today, recruiting, selecting, and resourcing a competent children's ministry director (or pastor) is one of the highest priorities for a church, especially a church plant that wants to attract young families.

What is the look and feel of "the front door" of the children's area? Do they have their own VIP team to welcome kids and reassure nervous parents the adults will take good care of them? Do the kids' pastor and workers in every age group exude calm and confidence, or do they emit an air of stress and drama? If parents sense even a whiff of chaos, you've seriously eroded, if not shattered, their trust in your church's leaders. The church members who brought them will be embarrassed, and the new family will find somewhere else to go the following week. Even if you're in a temporary situation like a school, pipe and drapes, partitions, and colorful, professionally made signs can do wonders to set a positive tone. Compliance issues must be top of mind, and a safe, secure identification and communication system is essential. We've said it's important to see every guest as someone handed to us by Jesus Himself. In the kids' ministry area, every child is being handed off by Jesus *and* the parents—and all three of them expect us to treat their kids with the utmost love and care.

- Station five: the auditorium. Before the service begins and people are finding their places, is the lighting too dark? Is it too glaringly bright? Is the background music setting the right mood? Some people come early to sit quietly to prepare their hearts, so the preservice prayer meeting needs to end well before the service begins. If the person is a guest, it will probably be disconcerting to hear someone speaking in tongues or praying down the fire of heaven!

What's the first thing that happens in the service? You may want to begin with a song, but very soon after that, people need to see a smiling face and hear a warm welcome. Years ago, I brought my mother to her first Spirit-filled service, and after it was over, she asked, "What was all that about, Michael?" With a catholic background, she had never seen people standing with their hands raised, their eyes closed, and mumbling things she couldn't understand. She said, "Why did they go into oblivion?" She's not the only one who is somewhat less than familiar with our style of worship, so we need to see the service through their eyes, too.

What decibel level is the sound? If you have Harry the Headbanger as your sound guy, he probably won't be sensitive to those who seldom attend rock concerts. If it's too loud, you'll lose some people over fifty, but if you dial it down a bit, you won't necessarily lose any younger people. The issue isn't what your sound guy prefers or even what you prefer. If you're guest-centric, you'll hear the music through the ears of those who attend for the first time.

The ethnic configuration of the worship team is important. People need to see at least one person who looks like them. It's almost impossible to build a church with diversity if the people on display in front of guests don't reflect who they are. Song selection is important. Don't introduce too many new songs too fast. Many pastors work with their worship leader to identify thirty or so excellent songs, and they let the worship leader make the selection each week. Of course, this list is regularly curated as new songs become available.

The sense of unity (or the lack of it) on the worship team is palpable to a lot of people, so character counts. Artists can be fragile, so the leader needs to have excellent interpersonal leadership skills in addition to musical acumen. To debrief each week, it's a good idea to have the worship team sit together to watch the video of their part of the service so they can critique themselves and grow in their proficiency.

It's helpful to ask your most dedicated worshippers and your leadership team to sit in the front rows to serve as visible and verbal examples for the rest of the congregation. Though this may not be a requirement, a warm compelling invitation is well in order. Similarly, I would also ask leaders to take notes when they listen to the message (in fact it's unthinkable that they wouldn't). This, too, is an example to those sitting near them that imparting and absorbing God's truth is very important. How do you ask them to sit in the front rows and take notes? It's easy. Just say, "Here's what I need from you," and spell it out. Explain the impact these simple steps can have on people as they share in worship. I hear some of you thinking, "Wow! That feels kind of controlling?" I hear ya, but I prefer to call it leadership.

In my experience with hundreds of pastors over decades, I'd report that the single most important tool they can use to improve the worship experience is a regular, FORMAL debrief. Emphasis on FORMAL! I'm not talking about a cursory, "How do you think it went yesterday, mate?" Here's how the rest of that conversation with the team goes:

"Good, I believe."

"Hey, Pastor, great last point in your message."

"Jan, wonderful harmony on that song."

"Yeah, it went well."

That level of analysis achieves one purpose: it avoids any hint of constructive criticism. A formal debrief means careful analysis, getting into details, and action points for improvement the next week. And in next week's debrief, the first item on the agenda is a look at how well the action points from the previous week were implemented. This method of analysis gives traction to substantive improvement and lowers the level of pastoral frustration. I've had more conversations than I can count with pastors who couldn't understand why their directives for improvement weren't followed. Nothing changed because the feedback wasn't clear enough, and even if it was, accountability was lacking. If problems persist, you have two problems: with your people and with your system. A formal debrief every week will shore up your system and clarify the expectations for your people.

The makeup of the team doing the debrief is a "choose your own adventure." It needs to include some people outside the worship team and the pastor so you can get objective input: the pastor, the worship leader, perhaps one of the people in the band or a singer, a deacon or an elder, the head usher, and maybe a group leader or two. You'll soon realize that some staff members and volunteers who aren't very musically skilled nonetheless have brilliant insights about the service. Value them, let them speak, and invite them often. One of the people in the meeting can be a roving observer who brings information about what's happening outside, in the lobby, and in the children's ministry. The debrief doesn't have to be in person with everyone sitting around a table. It can be on Zoom, or you can ask for written input from those who can't attend the meeting. You don't need to cover every topic every week. Create a monthly template that addresses a few things every week but other agenda items every other Sunday or once a month.

The pastor's sermon may be part of the debrief, or this may happen with a different set of people. The principle, however, is the same: the best way to improve is to receive honest and regular feedback. All of us have blind spots, and all of us can improve, even if we're known as skilled communicators. A disciple is a learner, and we never stop learning to serve the Master more effectively.

We need a system that promotes "constant and never-ending improvement": CANI. This rigorous and thorough debrief is, in my opinion, the best tool to max the Sunday experience.

The primary purpose of our worship is to please God with our praise and prayers. Our second purpose is to move the hearts of the people in the room—not just fill their minds but to bring them to "the throne of grace" to "obtain mercy and find grace to help in time of need" (Hebrews 4:16). The truth of Scripture is like a scalpel in the hands of a gifted surgeon. A few verses before, the writer reminds us, "For the word of God is living and powerful, and sharper than any two-edged sword, piercing even to the division of soul and spirit, and of joints and marrow, and is a discerner of the thoughts and intents of the heart. And there is no creature hidden from His sight, but all things are naked and open to the eyes of Him to whom we must give account" (vs. 12-13).

It's our task . . . it's our unspeakable privilege . . . to create an environment where every aspect of the service is that scalpel in God's loving hands. Our job is to take them to Him. When songs are too sophisticated or too wordy, they lose their power and leave people feeling confused and empty. The worship leader isn't there just to lead songs; it's to take people on a journey into the presence of Almighty God. The message isn't meant just to impress people with our rhetorical gifts; it's to be part of the answer to Paul's prayer that God would work so that "the eyes of your understanding being enlightened; that you may know what is the hope of His calling, what are the riches of the glory of His inheritance in the saints, and what is the exceeding greatness of His power toward us who believe, according to the working of His mighty power" (Ephesians 1:18-19). Nothing less than that!

Like the rest of us, pastors are creatures of habit. Some of the habits we've developed in our speaking skills are good ones, but undoubtedly, there are some that could use some improvement. I recommend pastors take courses in hermeneutics and homiletics every few years as refreshers. A fresh perspective will show up in how the Word of God is honored and delivered week after week.

Each of us has a preaching and teaching style. I want to say it doesn't matter what your style is because God will use you, and to some extent, that's true. Our task is to avoid getting in His way. To be an open channel of truth and grace, we need to first tap into the heart of God for ourselves so truth and grace overflow from us as we speak. We can't control the response, but the beauty and power of the message, and the ethos of the messenger, are inextricably linked to the level of openness of the hearers.

It's a good idea to go back to basics. What is the gospel? In the Roman world, an announcement would be made when a new emperor or king came to the throne. He promised peace throughout the land, and the people believed this was "Good News." The Good News of the gospel is that we have a crucified and risen King. He didn't just come from a foreign province to take the throne; He came from heaven to earth to establish a new kingdom. Am I saying the gospel isn't justification by faith? Not at all. But I'm saying it's more than that—the One who justifies is the Lord of All, the King of Glory, the One who deserves our love and loyalty, especially because we were just set free from the prison of our sin and declared righteous in His sight; we have been adopted into the royal family and invited to be junior partners in the family business of bringing Christ's reign "on earth as it is in heaven." Our gospel centers on justification, but we're justified by the King... and that matters in our security, our motivations, and the way we relate to those inside and outside God's family. In His first message in the synagogue in His hometown of Nazareth, Jesus read from the scroll of Isaiah:

> *"The Spirit of the Lord is upon Me,*
> *Because He has anointed Me*
> *To preach the gospel to the poor;*
> *He has sent Me to heal the brokenhearted,*
> *To proclaim liberty to the captives*
> *And recovery of sight to the blind,*
> *To set at liberty those who are oppressed;*
> *To proclaim the acceptable year of the Lord."*
> —Luke 4:18-19

All of the miracles were signs of the new kingdom, and all of the parables exposed the secrets of the kingdom. From first to last, it's all about the kingdom, and it's a powerful one. Paul reminded the Corinthians, "And my speech and my preaching were not with persuasive words of human wisdom, but in demonstration of the Spirit and of power, that your faith should not be in the wisdom of men but in the power of God" (1 Corinthians 2:4-5). Where does this power come from? I believe we need to spend as much time asking God to make our message each week real to our own hearts as we spend preparing a beautiful, powerful, coherent message. We pray the Word in before we speak it out.

Young pastors often try to say far too much. (I know I definitely did and sometimes still do! Ha!!) Maybe they've studied hard and they don't want any point to go to waste, or maybe they really believe the volume of words makes a difference, or maybe they're just insecure and don't know when to quit. Sooner or later, we learn that a dump truck isn't useful as the last instrument in our preparation. It's useful to bring in lots of raw material, but as we refine our message, we need the tools of a sculptor to chip away everything that isn't necessary to make the points. And remember, we want our entire service to be guest-centric. That doesn't mean we can't talk about deep truths, but skilled communicators are able to make hard bones of truth digestible.

The introduction—the first five minutes—of the sermon sets the tone and lets people know the message is for them. The goal is to connect with them like you were sitting down with them at a coffee shop. If I've never spoken at a particular church before, I take seven to ten minutes. It's that important. I share some of my story, I'm appropriately vulnerable, and I throw in some self-deprecating humor. If pastors craft their introductions well, it's like sharpening an ax. It takes time to get it sharp, but it cuts far, far better than a blunt ax. The introduction prepares hearts to pay close attention because it communicates, "I think this guy really gets me!" I often ask questions: "Have you ever thought . . . ?" "Have you ever felt . . . ?" Here's a benchmark: Do people feel known and loved at the end of your introduction? Do they have a strong sense of anticipation of what's coming in the message? Do they trust that you're genuine and not a con? A good introduction answers at least one of those questions.

When Jesus spoke to Jewish audiences, He often said, "It is written . . .," and quoted Scripture. But when He spoke to non-Jewish audiences who didn't have a concept of the authority of Scripture, He told stories to explain His points and earn the trust of the people. What does that mean for us? In the last couple of decades, and especially in the younger generations, we've seen a huge increase in the number of "nones," those who may or may not be atheists or agnostics, but they have no affiliation with any organized religion. So, even churches in a Bible Belt are seeing more people come who have little to no background in the Scriptures or the basics of the faith. Each week, then, we need to teach God's Word in a way that speaks to the honest doubts and ignorance of many people in the room. That means we need insight to put ourselves in their shoes and teach the Word in a way that moves them. We don't back down from the truth. Not at all. But we fine-tune our message so we don't make as many assumptions about the people listening. If we'll tailor our message to speak to those without much spiritual background, they'll invite their friends to join them in listening to us.

Many pastors are disappointed because their people listen and nod during the sermon, but they don't do anything to apply it. That's always a challenge, but we can at least move the needle toward action. When I speak, I begin with the end in mind. In the introduction, usually after I've shared a vulnerable story about my brokenness, I'll say something like, "At the end of the message, I'm going to ask God to do something wonderful in the hearts of people in the room today who are in despair over their brokenness. If you're bumping along the bottom spiritually, I believe today is your day. Today you can humble your heart before God, acknowledge how much you need Him, and rededicate yourself to Him. Or you may be visiting here for the first time or the first time in a long time. This is your day too, so get ready." Then I proceed with the message. In the middle of the sermon, I refer again to the fact that I'm going to ask them to respond at the end. I'm priming the pump, helping them anticipate a positive response. By the time we get to the end and I ask them to take a step of faith, I've woven the call to action throughout the message—it's not a sermon with a disconnected response bolted on the backend. If I've prepared them, they aren't surprised, and they don't feel manipulated. They knew what was coming, and they respond without feeling pressured or tricked. The Word of God inherently calls people to choose: this gate or that one, this road or that one, this house or that one, this Lord or that one.

> The Word of God inherently calls people to choose: this gate or that one, this road or that one, this house or that one, this Lord or that one.

We want people to receive gifts of grace, love, power, and wisdom from God during the service. Some pastors have created opportunities for rich spiritual experiences during their worship service. For instance, my great friend Greg Surratt is the now-retired pastor of Seacoast Church in Mt. Pleasant, South Carolina. At the end of the services at his church, people can, if they want, move to one of four stations in the corners of the room: at one, a candle is burning as they pray for someone they love; at another, a cross speaks to them of Christ's glad sacrifice to pay for their sins and give them new life, and there, they can kneel in thankfulness or offer a prayer of confession and be assured of God's forgiveness; at a third, they share the bread and the cup of Communion; and at the fourth station, people can ask for prayer and have someone on the prayer team pray for them on the spot.

The first week or two when Greg offered these opportunities, I'm sure some people felt a bit uncomfortable . . . simply because it was new. But after a few weeks, it became a new tradition, a treasured moment in every service. Pastor, people may forget the points in the sermon before they get to lunch, but they won't forget that you created a place where God met them in their moment of need.

Every church, no matter the denomination and history, can create moments like this. Spirit-filled churches may enlist leaders to operate in their gifts. They can provide opportunities for those who are struggling with direction to talk to someone with a prophetic gift, someone who is sick to meet with a leader with the gift of healing, or someone who feels spiritually and relationally stuck can meet with a leader with the gifts of wisdom and discernment.

As I've met with pastors who have created wonderfully rich worship moments where people connect with God, I've come to the conclusion that the Holy Spirit is making a comeback! Of course, He never went anywhere, but it seems the Spirit of God is moving in our leaders to give them a vision of creating tender moments between God and the people who seek Him. God rejoices with those who rejoice, and His heart breaks when we're brokenhearted. We need to get in touch with His immense love, compassion, and care, and when we do, we'll create space for our people to get in touch with Him too.

Some pastors hear about churches that are creating these deeply moving moments, and they claim, "There's just not room in the service for one more thing!" I would push back and ask, "What are we trying to do in our services? Isn't creating an opportunity for people to connect with God's heart pretty high on our priority list?" If we don't have time for these moments, we probably need to take some scissors to some other parts of our services so we can make room. After all, it's His church, and they're His people. Surely we can be flexible enough to foster this vital connection.

Wise pastors pepper their messages with encouragement for people to study the Bible and pray on their own. One of the greatest gifts we can give our people is the motivation and skills to be self-feeding. In your messages, talk about the importance of regular Bible reading and time in prayer, and provide resources to help them connect with God Monday through Saturday.

Maxing your Sunday isn't about size; it's about the Guest Golden Rule: treating people who walk through your doors the way you'd want to be treated if you were coming for the first time. Do the hard work of analysis, get honest and regular feedback, and identify your blind spots so you can reach more people and enlist them in the kingdom.

Sunday isn't just about the music and the sermon. XLR8's promise is that if you curate your Sunday with guests in mind—making it abundantly clear that the next step for guests is Growth Track—you will turn your Sunday into an on-ramp to genuine discipleship.

Formula 1 owners, engineers, mechanics, crews, and drivers are meticulous in analyzing every aspect of the car's design and performance. The stakes for us are infinitely higher.

PIT STOP

We've already examined what needs to happen to create a VIP team to engage and welcome people. Now, take some time to evaluate the stations from your lobby to your auditorium.

- Station four: the children's area.
- What is the look and feel of "the front door" of the children's area?
- Do they have their own VIP team to welcome kids and reassure nervous parents the adults will take good care of them?
- Do the kids' pastor and workers in every age group exude calm and confidence, or do they emit an air of stress and drama?
- Station five: the auditorium.
- Before the service begins and people are finding their places, is the lighting too dark? Is it too glaringly bright?

- Is the background music setting the right mood?
- Are you finished with prayer in the auditorium at least fifteen minutes before the service starts?

Consider your sermons. What difference would it make (or does it make) to:

- Spend as much time praying the message into your heart as you spend studying for the delivery?
- Give more attention to your introductions to connect more effectively and prepare people to take action?
- Communicate the gospel of the kingdom?
- Relate to those who have little to no spiritual background?
- Create experiences within the service?
- Regularly and rigorously debrief so you can pursue continuous and never-ending improvement?

"Giving thanks to the Father who has qualified us to be partakers of the inheritance of the saints in the light. He has delivered us from the power of darkness and conveyed us into the kingdom of the Son of His love, in whom we have redemption through His blood, the forgiveness of sins."

—Colossians 1:12-14

FOURTH GEAR: MOBILIZE FOR MISSION

What is it with you Americans? You drive on the wrong side of the road! When we took our family on vacation in California, it wasn't exactly what you see pictured in travel ads. I was driving on the Pacific Coast Highway near Carmel when our sweet, obedient children turned feral. Words of correction, encouragement, and nuclear warnings weren't enough, so I pulled over, turned around, and read each one the riot act one by one! When I'd finished my tirade, I pulled out into the highway—some idiot was coming right at me on the wrong side of the road! It didn't take me long to realized I was actually the idiot! My boiling anger and skyrocketing blood pressure had short-circuited my prefrontal cortex, and all reason had been left on the side of the road where I'd attempted to rein in our errant children! I had reverted to Aussie rules of the road . . . with almost catastrophic results.

Have you ever been there? No, I don't mean pulling into the wrong lane of traffic, though you might have had that experience. I'm talking about reverting to past perspectives instead of living in reality in the moment. Sure you have . . . we all have. It's easy to put our brains on autopilot and miss the true mission of the church. There is a big difference between the challenge to "come to church" and the commission to "become the church"!

Jesus, Paul, and other New Testament writers made it crystal clear that every believer has a special role in the body of Christ. Luke tells us that Jesus's mission wasn't limited to Him and the Twelve: "After these things the Lord appointed seventy others also, and sent them two by two before His face into every city and place where He Himself was about to go. Then He said to them, 'The harvest truly is great, but the laborers are few; therefore pray the Lord of the harvest to send out laborers into His harvest'" (Luke 10:1-2). Jesus is the Lord of the harvest, and if we follow Him, we'll join Him in the harvest fields. In His most famous sermon, Jesus said that we're light and salt—light that attracts and shows the way and salt that preserves and makes food delicious. We're to be lighthouses that broadcast light widely so many people will "see the light," and our communication of the gospel of grace needs to be warm, loving, and hopeful . . . which sounds delicious to those who hear! That message wasn't just for the Twelve. It's for all believers. It's for you, me, and everyone in our churches.

Peter drew from God's pronouncement to the children of Israel just before Moses went up Mt. Sinai to receive the Ten Commandments. He wrote to the believers who had run for their lives from persecution, "But you are a chosen generation, a royal priesthood, a holy nation, His own special people, that you may proclaim the praises of Him who called you out of darkness into His marvelous light; who once were not a people but are now the people of God, who had not obtained mercy but now have obtained mercy" (I Peter 2:9-10). We aren't divided into an upper caste of pastors, teachers, evangelists, apostles, and prophets and a lower class of the rest who sit on the sidelines and cheer them on. No, all of us are chosen by Almighty God to be royal priests. That's a very odd thing because the king's family and the priests were always separate, but in Christ, we're both—children of the King appointed to represent Him to people wherever we go (that's the role of priests). We are "special people." Another translation of the passage in Exodus and here is that we are God's "treasure." We aren't cheerleaders, we aren't slaves, and we aren't hired hands. We're children who serve in our Father's shop. And what do we do? We tell everyone who will listen that God "has called us out of darkness and into His marvelous light." In other words, we announce the Good News of the crucified and risen King who takes away the sins of the world, credits our account with the very righteousness of Christ, and says to each of us, "Follow me."

Paul used a number of metaphors to get at the idea that all believers are on mission with Jesus. Amazingly (to the Jews and Gentiles of the first century and to the bitter divisions in our own), he wrote to the Ephesians that the cross of Christ has "broken down the middle wall of separation" at the Temple which was a barrier to Gentiles, "that He might reconcile them both to God in one body through the cross, thereby putting to death the enmity" (Ephesians 2:14, 16). In other words, the cross kills hatred—or maybe more accurately, our genuine experience of Christ's loving sacrifice softens our hearts and infuses us with His toward those who disagree with us, despise us, and hold views we find unacceptable. Paul then combines the metaphors of a family and a temple: "Now, therefore, you are no longer strangers and foreigners, but fellow citizens with the saints and members of the household of God, having been built on the foundation of the apostles and prophets, Jesus Christ Himself being the chief cornerstone, in whom the whole building, being fitted together, grows into a holy temple in the Lord, in whom you also are being built together for a dwelling place of God in the Spirit" (vs. 19-22). And to the Corinthians, he wrote the stunning comment that each of us individually and all believers collectively are "the temple of the Holy Spirit," the place where heaven and earth meet (1 Corinthians 6:19).

One of the reasons the church grew in the first three centuries after the resurrection from less than one percent to as much as fifty percent of the population of the Roman Empire is that all believers (or virtually all) saw themselves as ministers of the gospel and servants of their neighbors. For them, being a believer in Christ changed their entire identity, motivations, and interactions. It should be no different for believers in every generation. There's certainly nothing wrong with moving chairs, setting up the sound system, and serving in a hundred different capacities within the walls of the church (and indeed, every believer should be actively involved in serving within the House of God), but our God-given mission is to advance Christ's kingdom into every community, every neighborhood, every home, and every heart. Nothing else and nothing less.

> It should be no different for believers in every generation.

Jesus had in mind a fully alive family of God functioning in the fullness of the Holy Spirit and all of the gifts to reach a lost and dying world and call them to be genuine disciples who follow Jesus wherever He leads them. We're often focused on *seating* capacity, but God is focused on *sending* capacity. Let me offer a few concepts that I hope will refocus our attention:

THIS IS WAR

I believe many people in our churches have been lulled to sleep by a satanic lullaby, so we're not awake to God's clear calling. Rather than being active to *become* the church in all its radiance, beauty, and power, too many of us are content with *coming* to church. Our primary metric is the number of people in chairs on Sunday mornings, not how many are engaging people with grace and truth in every aspect of their lives. I don't mean to be harsh, but that's no different from the Rotary Club. We need a fresh jolt of understanding of what's at stake and what we're up against. In his book, *The Fight*, John White pulls no punches:

> *You have established a new relationship with the powers of darkness. Whatever you were before you were a Christian . . . you are now a sworn foe of the legions of hell. Have no delusions about their reality or their hostility, but do not fear them. The God inside you terrifies them. They cannot hurt you..., but they can still seduce, and they will try. They will also oppose you as you obey Christ. . . . if you are serious about Christ being your Lord and God, you can expect opposition.*[4]

One of the primary ways to understand the gospel is Christus Victor, that Jesus has won the battle over sin, death, and Satan. Paul described Jesus' victory in his letter to the Colossians: "And you, being dead in your trespasses and the uncircumcision of your flesh, He has made alive together with Him, having forgiven you all trespasses, having wiped out the handwriting of requirements that was against us, which was contrary to us. And He has taken it out of the way, having nailed it to the cross. Having disarmed principalities and powers, He made a public spectacle of them, triumphing over them in

---

4 John White, *The Fight* (Downers Grove: Intervarsity Press, 1976), p. 5.

it" (Colossians 2:13-15). Jesus has already triumphed, and in the paradox of paradoxes, He won His victory through His sacrificial death.

Let me offer a few practical applications we can train into the lives of our people:

- Pray for your top three—Ask every person in your church to identify three people who aren't yet believers and commit to pray regularly that God would move in their hearts and they would embrace Christ.
- Unwrap the gifts of the Spirit—Many people in our congregations assume evangelism is reserved for the paid professionals. Not so. As people operate in their gifts, no matter what they are, they become more alive, more sensitive to the Spirit, and more assertive in taking the initiative to share the gospel with others. The gifts aren't just to be used inside the walls of the church.
- Bring instead of invite—This is the same principle we discussed about members of the VIP team going with guests to drop kids off at the kids' ministry and inviting them to sit together in the service. The battle for souls is waged in many different ways, but one of them is when we provide easy outs for people. Satan loves that. But if we offer to bring them with us, we've taken away one of the barriers, and we've won at least a skirmish in the fight.
- Release the intercessors—This is important, but fair warning: I've seen more than my fair share of strangeness in intercessory ministries. Aside from off-the-wall expectations, some people have used this time for gossip. So, I'm all for it, but only if it's led by a mature leader who can give direction, be an example of believing prayer, and rein in the weirdness. And now, back to our regularly scheduled content: Spiritual warfare is waged in prayer, and the hearts of unbelievers are softened as the Spirit awakens them to see the truth of the gospel. Ask prayer groups

to make praying for unbelievers a regular part of their time of intercession, ask small groups to pray for their top three (they might use an empty chair to visualize those they're praying for), and pray in the service that God would open hearts.
- Believe in and for God-encounters—God does, in fact, work in mysterious ways. We may call them "coincidences," but there's no such thing under the sovereignty of God. People may have dreams or visions about Jesus, or He may overwhelm them with a sense of His presence. There's no telling what God will do to draw sinners to Himself.

KNOW YOUR TARGETS

We've established that a good goal for guest cards is three to four percent of those in attendance each week. In this case, a worthy goal is for thirty to forty percent of attenders to be mobilized to share their faith regularly or at the least bring people to church.

EMPOWER YOUR EVANGELISTS

Some percentage of every church body has the gift of evangelism. (I guesstimate ten percent.) If you put some smelling salts under their noses, they wake up and become energized to initiate conversations that make an eternal impact. Quite often, we highlight the person who has come to faith and ask the person for a testimony (and rightly so), but we also need to highlight the one who led that person to Christ. I recommend that pastors invite those who seem to have this gift to a meeting and tell them, "You have no idea how much you mean to this church and to the Lord. You touch people in ways most of us don't, and we really need you. I want you to know that I'm praying for you. Whatever you need as you reach out to those who aren't yet believers, let me know. I'll do all I can to give you what you need." I might add,

"If you bring ten people over the next month, I'll move Mrs. O'Malley out of her seat on the third row so you and your friends can sit there!" (Unless Mrs. O'Malley gets mobilized, and then she can stay!)

And remember that new believers are often the best evangelists because they still have good friends who aren't Christians. So when a rough, gnarly, tatted-up guy trusts in Jesus, give him a vision to have an impact on his buddies. When a bunch of them come and you move Mrs. O'Malley out of her regular seat, even she will be thrilled! (Mmmm, hopefully!)

ENLIST THE ENTIRE CHURCH

The last thing Jesus said needs to be our first priority: "Go and make disciples." That wasn't the directive for pastors, a few "radicals," or hired guns from out of town. It's for all of us. In the passages at the beginning of this chapter, Jesus, Peter, and Paul called all of us to live out our new identity as "called out ones." They're saying the same thing to us today. Most people have gotten into an entrenched mental habit of believing they can never be soul winners. We need to restore the vision, the mission, and the calling.

It's easy to come up with excuses. We do it all the time. Just before Jesus sent the seventy out, He encountered three men who had conditions following Him. The first one proclaimed, "Lord, I will follow You wherever you go."

But Jesus saw through his bravado and told him, "Foxes have holes and birds of the air have nests, but the Son of Man has nowhere to lay His head." The implication is that he actually had limits on his commitment. He wanted to stay in nice hotels if he went with Jesus!

The second one indicated that he wanted to follow Jesus, but his condition seemed very reasonable: "Lord, let me first go and bury my father."

In that culture, it was likely that his father was old but wasn't dead, and the man was asking for an extended time off. Jesus told him, "Let the dead bury their own dead, but you go and preach the kingdom of God."

And another man promised, "Lord, I will follow," but he had a different condition: "but let me first go and bid them farewell who are at my house."

Jesus replied, "No one, having put his hand to the plow, and looking back, is fit for the kingdom of God" (Luke 9:57-62). The man was torn between loyalty to his family and loyalty to Jesus.

I don't think we should wag our heads at those three men . . . because we're much like them, or at least I am. Our conditions may be different, but the process of becoming a true disciple of Jesus involves identifying our conditions and replacing them with repentance and obedience. What are some of our conditions? We could probably list dozens, such as, "I'm really busy," "I don't know enough," "My life has been a wreck," "My kids need me more than ever," "My parents are old and need my help," and on and on. So, pastor, first examine your own heart to see any excuses that promise you can remain in control of your future or that God owes you because you've earned blessings by your hard work. When you identify them, repent, bask in God's forgiveness, and recommit yourself to His agenda. Then become a student of our culture and identify the common roadblocks and detours that keep your people from moving forward. Explain that being God's partner in the family business is the greatest honor ever bestowed on anyone, and give them clear and concrete steps to reach the lost and care for the least.

Every person who has been truly saved has a heart to bring others to the Savior. It's the most natural and normal thing in the world because, as Paul wrote in his prayer for the Christians in Colossae: We are "giving thanks to the Father who has qualified us to be partakers of the inheritance of the saints in the light. He has delivered us from the power of darkness and conveyed us into the kingdom of the Son of His love, in whom we have redemption through His blood, the forgiveness of sins" (Colossians 1:12-14). As one pastor said, "If that doesn't ring your bell, you might still be asleep." When our sports team has won, we want to tell everyone about it. How much more do we want to tell people when our Savior has won the greatest victory in history!

> Every person who has been truly saved has a heart to bring others to the Savior.

God has given us Himself in the person of Jesus, He has given us the Word of God that is sharper than a sword, He has given us the Holy Spirit to lead and empower us to represent Him, and He has given us marching orders to take the gospel to every human heart. He has put us in the most perfect and powerful Lamborghini with incredible potential, but we're driving it around backstreets like it's a golf cart. (No offense to our Floridian retiree friends. I love golf carts!) We can do better than that. We must do better than that.

EXEMPLIFY THE WORK

One of the most inspiring things we can do for our people is show them the fruit of our preaching in our own lives. This means telling them about someone we've led to Christ or pointing to people in the audience we've brought. If we want our people to be soul-winners, we need to be soul-winners, which means carving out time to be in environments with unbelievers so we can have real relationships with at least a few of them. If we want our people to be bringers instead of inviters, we need to bring people and let people know we've listened to our own sermons.

Leading a church can easily be an all-consuming task, and the longer we've been pastors, the easier it is to have our time consumed with meeting with Christians (staff members, board members, people who come for counseling, key volunteers, and so on), solving problems, and our administrative load. I get it—being a pastor is very demanding, but we need to step back and reevaluate our schedules. We need to prioritize time in social situations so we can have relaxed, conversational times with people who don't know the Lord. But we need to be careful: If they sense that they're targets to hit instead of people to know and love, they won't sense the love of Jesus. I know pastors who go to the golf course each week without partners so they can join one, two, or three guys they don't already know. Others coach their kids' sports teams or play on a city league team, go to the same coffee shop to interact with the barista and the regulars, join local service clubs, become chaplains for the police force, and other creative ways to regularly rub shoulders with people who need the Lord. The options are endless. Find one.

When I go out to eat, I try to always engage the wait staff. I always begin with a little "over the top" enthusiastic greeting: "Hey, thank you so much for serving us today! I really appreciate it." They're used to people grumbling about the food being cold, the water glass being empty, or the check didn't come fast enough, so a warm, friendly greeting sets the tone. After a little interaction about drinks or appetizers, I ask, "Tell me, what's your name?" When I hear the name, I repeat it in the next question, which has a strike rate of about eighty percent: "Are you in school? Do you work full-time or part-time?"

Sometimes a lady will say, "Full-time. I'm a single mom, and I need all the work I can get." My response is, "Oh man, you're a real hero! Your kids are so blessed to have you!" If the person says, "I'm still in school," I ask, "Great! What are you studying?" When he or she tells me, I try to connect, maybe like this: "Third year of psychology—I'm sure you're learning a lot about the people you serve every day!" Then I follow up: "When you graduate, what do you want to do?" By about the fifth question, I've made a real connection. I've probably taken enough of their time at this point, so I wait to reconnect later, and then I may say, "I'm a believer in Jesus. How can I pray for you?" I've done this in the middle of New York City and in country towns in Alabama. Genuine compassion is attractive anywhere. When I offer to pray, about one out of fifty says, "That's alright. I'm good." The rest are both surprised and glad for me to pray for them, sometimes right there at the table. If I'm with a pastor (and I'm always with a pastor!), I'll say, "Have you met Pastor James? He pastors a wonderful church right here in town." This gives the pastor an entrée to talk about his church and offer to take the person there the next week. Yeah, I know. I'm an extrovert, so you may not do it exactly like I do, but you can do it in your own way, and I guarantee that God will use your initiative.

EQUIP THE SAINTS

When our goal is reduced to filling enough seats, having good enough music, and preaching a good enough sermon, we've missed God's heart for the world. I know none of us would ever say that's good enough, but we work so hard to get Sunday right that our minds gradually cut a rut that leaves us riveted on that event to the detriment of everything else. Our job, Paul told the Ephesians, is to equip the saints to do the ministry, not to do it for them. You may not have had that problem, but it has certainly been part of my story in ministry. The things I'm writing in these chapters are hard-won principles.

In many churches, basic training in how to talk to unbelievers about Christ is missing. If you ask one hundred people in churches across America, Australia, and the world if they would like to be soul-winners, ninety-nine would say, "Yes!" But there's a problem. Many of those ninety-nine haven't been trained to make a clear, coherent, attractive presentation of the gospel, and many haven't been challenged to talk to unbelievers about their faith. A recent Lifeway survey found that forty-seven percent of unchurched people would be glad to discuss religious beliefs if a Christian wanted to talk with them about it, and another thirty-one percent would listen to a presentation without the give-and-take of a discussion. That's almost eight out of ten who have opened the doors of their hearts to listen to us! In spite of this openness, four in ten have never had a Christian talk to them about how to become a follower of Jesus.[5] (I would imagine the numbers in Australia are similar.)

My friend Josh Howard helps lead a movement that is currently discipling 300,000 people in India (that's not a typo), mostly from Hindu backgrounds. He has a strategy of rapid evangelism and rapid multiplication. He told me that his leaders teach people within days of their conversion to share a ninety-second testimony: three adjectives before you came to Christ, what He did in saving you, and three adjectives after you believed in Him. If I follow that model, my testimony would be:

> *"I lacked any sense of purpose, I was frustrated that I wasn't living up to my potential, and I covered the pain with alcohol, drugs, and immoral relationships. But when Jesus came into*

---

[5] "Christians Don't Share Faith with Unchurched Friends," Aaron Earls, Lifeway, September 9, 2021, https://research.lifeway.com/2021/09/09/christians-dont-share-faith-with-unchurched-friends/

my life, I was filled to the brim with purpose, hope, and love every day. I no longer self-medicate to cover the pain because God has healed and restored me from the inside out. I often pinch myself when I realize I get to live this full, abundant life in Christ!" I can then add... *"That's my story. Do you have a story like that?"*

How easy was that? So easy, but most believers haven't been trained to do anything like this, so when they think of opening their mouths to talk to a co-worker, neighbor, or family member, their brains short out and they talk about something else entirely.

When can pastors train their people in one-to-one evangelism? Most of them have a set of series they preach every year: relationships, giving and finances, and something creative like an at-the-movies series. I'd add another one: a few weeks on soul-winning, with the messages backed up and reinforced in small groups.

Quite often, sensitive people ask, "But what if the people don't want to talk to me? And worse, what if they reject me?"

I want to tell them, "So what? You've offered them the greatest treasure anyone can ever receive. There's no shame in that! And besides, Jesus was so rejected that He was executed on a Roman cross, so you don't need to feel too bad about someone who doesn't want to talk to you about your faith."

An essential part of training people to share their faith (and an equally essential aspect of their motivation to follow Jesus) is making the gospel clear. I'm not talking about a seminary-level course on the various theories of atonement (though that might be a good idea for staff and high-level leaders). I'm talking about the fundamental concept of salvation by grace alone, through faith alone, in Christ alone. Let me give some context: A few decades ago, many churches misconstrued the gospel with legalism. Yes, you had to have faith, but you really needed to follow all the rules to be accepted by God (and us). This teaching crushed the joy out of experiencing the joy of God's grace. More recently, this concept has morphed into moralism—no more rigid rules, but we prove we're acceptable by being "good enough" people. In the Western world, that's the dominant philosophy and warped theology, even in many churches, and certainly in the hearts of most people. Why would I say that? Because the human heart longs to prove itself. Grace tells us we can't prove ourselves, no matter how hard we try. So salvation isn't by what we've done; it's by what Christ has done for us. (Gosh, I so needed to get this as a young believer!) Before Paul gets to his brilliant and brief explanation of salvation in his letter to the Ephesians, he makes sure to cut the legs out from under legalism or moralism. We aren't "pretty good people who need a little help from God"—we "were dead in trespasses and sins . . . fulfilling the desires of the flesh and of the mind, and were by nature children of wrath, just as the others" (Ephesians 2:1, 3). We often identify the desires of the flesh as stealing, adultery, murder, and lying, but those weren't the desires of the flesh for the Pharisees. Their sin was insisting they could follow enough rules and be good enough to earn God's favor. So there are two categories of desires of the flesh: immorality and self-righteousness. Paul then describes the incredible mercy of God and summarizes: "For by grace you have been saved through faith, and that not of yourselves; it is the gift of God, not of works, lest anyone should boast. For we are His workmanship, created in Christ Jesus for good works, which God prepared beforehand that we should walk in them" (vs. 8-10). Grace alone, faith alone, Christ alone. And when God's grace takes root in our hearts, we want to do good works to love and serve people, not to get love and approval but from a heart overflowing with love and approval. As you preach and teach a clear gospel message, your people will pick it up, emulate your language, and communicate more clearly with other people.

OPEN YOUR EYES

Sometimes, people who need Christ are right under our noses (or roofs), and we need to sit up and notice. At the outbreak of World War II, when the Nazis and Soviets invaded Poland from each direction, German businessman Oskar Schindler moved to Krakow to make a fortune from the war. He had joined the Nazi party to prove his loyalty, but the staff at his factory were Jews . . . they were displaced, so they were available and cheap. The Nazis rounded up all the Jews and forced them into an inner city ghetto, and they began shipping them to Auschwitz, a nearby death camp. Schindler arranged to protect his workers so his operation could proceed unhindered, but he soon realized his plan wasn't just good for business—he was saving innocent lives. Through an elaborate ruse, he managed to save about 1,100 Jews from extermination. It was one of the most daring and generous acts of the war, but near the end, he thought about all those he hadn't been able to save, and to his bookkeeper and partner in the scheme, Itzhak Stern, he moaned, "I could have gotten more out. I could have got more. I don't know. If I'd just . . . I could have got more."

Stern reminded him, "Oskar, there are eleven hundred people who are alive because of you." (Pointing out the window.) "Look at them."

Schindler was inconsolable. "If I'd made more money. . . . I threw away so much money. You have no idea. If I'd just . . ."

Again, Stern offered a better perspective: "There will be generations because of what you did."

At this, Schindler explodes, "I didn't do enough!"

"You did so much."

Schindler looked at his car and, in a pang of self-reflection, commented, "This car. Goethe would have bought the car. Why did I keep the car? Ten people right there. Ten people. Ten more people." He then picked the Nazi lapel pin from his suit coat and said, "This pin. Two people. This is gold. Two more people. He would have given me two for it, at least one. One more person. A person, Stern. For this." He broke down in tears and spoke into the emotional gloom, "I could have gotten one more person . . . and I didn't! And I . . . I didn't!"[6]

Jesus knew that He had come from eternity past and would live in eternity future, but time on earth is limited and precious. He told His disciples, "I must work the works of Him who sent Me while it is day; the night is coming when no one can work" (John 9:4). For Paul, there was always a sense of urgency to take the gospel throughout the known world. In his second letter to the Corinthians, he first reminded them that they lived in a new kingdom under a new King, one who had given them (all of them and all of us) a noble job: "Therefore, if anyone is in Christ, he is a new creation; old things have passed away; behold, all things have become new. Now all things are of God, who has reconciled us to Himself through Jesus Christ, and has given us the ministry of reconciliation, that is, that God was in Christ reconciling the world to Himself, not imputing their trespasses to them, and has committed to us the word of reconciliation" (2 Corinthians 5:17-19). Then Paul reminded them of their identity and prodded them to action: "Now then, we are ambassadors for Christ, as though God were pleading through us: we implore you on Christ's behalf, be reconciled to God" (vs. 20). He was imploring believers to implore unbelievers to believe.

---

6 *Schindler's List*, Directed by Steven Spielberg, Amblin Entertainment, 1993.

CELEBRATE THE BRINGERS

As I mentioned, it's glorious to honor people who have recently come to faith: "This is Bob. He just got out of prison. He was in for twenty-five years, and he's only twenty-eight years old. He was in for armed robbery and murder, but praise God, Bob found Jesus, and he's turned his life over to Him. Don't pay attention to the naked lady tattoo on his neck. He promised to have clothes put on her next week. Let's give a cheer for Jesus and Bob!" Yes, it's wonderful to celebrate Bob, but not many people are like Bob. If we only highlight murderers, addicts, and Mafia bosses, we run the risk of communicating to our people that sharing the gospel is always very dramatic, and in fact, it's a dangerous proposition! If you want to highlight Bob, that's great, but also be sure to highlight other new believers like Nevil and Norma the Normal, Sarah the Safe, and Kendra the Kind.

Another mistake is to give too much attention to celebrities and sports stars. We sometimes make such a fuss about them that it appears they're giving Jesus credibility! This is based on the lie that a puny human being who has temporary success in a brief stage in life but is a vapor that will vanish in a relative instant is someone Jesus needs on His side. A second lie is that when a star joins a church, it will automatically grow. This takes our eyes off Jesus and on these people as the source of joy, love, and power. To be sure, the up-and-outs need Jesus every bit as much as the down-and-outs. Jesus met with Nicodemus as well as lepers and prostitutes; Paul reminded the Corinthians that "not many [of you were] mighty, not many noble" (1 Corinthians 1:26) have trusted in Jesus—which means that some believers in the church in Corinth were mighty and noble, but they weren't the backbone of the church. We need to reach and engage every person because everyone is a treasure in God's sight . . . and should be in ours.

We need to reach and engage every person because everyone is a treasure in God's sight... and should be in ours.

It sends a powerful and right message when we celebrate those who brought people to Christ. For instance, I might say in a service, "Today, I want Tony to stand. Tony has a tender heart for people who don't know Jesus. He and his wife Sarah met Steve and Alice, told them about Jesus, and they came to faith. Isn't that incredible? Steve and Alice, please stand. [Applause and cheers.] Steve and Alice are friends with James and Nancy. They shared the gospel with them, and James and Nancy trusted in Jesus. James and Nancy, please stand up. [More applause and cheers.] Steve and Alice invited James and Nancy to their small group, and now James and Nancy are leading a group, too! That's marvelous, isn't it?" (Even more applause and cheers.] This chain of faith sends a powerful, positive message to the entire congregation.

Now, pastor, before you get down on yourself because you can't think of any such "gospel chain" in your church, listen up! I want you to know that you can actually see outcomes just like this! As I'm penning (well, typing actually) these words, I'm being moved to tears for you! I sense a surge of faith for you, and I'm praying that God will infuse fresh confidence into your heart right now!

Many of us pastors have seasons where we lack faith in our people to lead others to Christ (they're really God's people, but you get what I mean). We didn't plan on having reduced faith, but it happened over time because we weren't seeing much evangelistic fruit throughout our congregations. But that can change. The transformation takes an accurate analysis of the problem, wisdom in crafting a plan to train and engage church attenders, setting an example, and celebrating the right things in the services.

I've had to learn these lessons, and I learned them the hard way. For a season, my own evangelism gift became stale and forgotten. I saw the fruit of numerical growth, but it was "faux fruit," people coming from other churches to ours. I thought it was my job to tell our people to bring their friends to church where I'd preach to them. There's nothing wrong with our people saying to friends, "Come and see," but the calling of every believer is to represent the crucified and risen King accurately as we become light and salt.

XLR8's promise is that mobilizing your people for mission will bring more people to church, more will receive Christ and be baptized, more will get into groups, and more of those who are mobilized will become leaders. Not bad. Not bad at all.

On Formula 1 teams, there are no spectators, no hangers-on. Every person is completely dedicated and brings their best every day, whether it's planning, practice, fine-tuning the car and the pit stops, or on race day. In the same way, every member of the body of Christ is assigned a crucial role in the kingdom. We trust the Lord of the harvest to send forth laborers into His harvest. Pastors, our role is to call greatness out of our people as laborers in God's harvest field.

PIT STOP

Though the greatest impact on a church's trajectory and latent potential of the church today and always is the mobilization of the body of Christ on mission, there are other related factors. With now just over half of *XLR8* behind you, let's take this time out to think about all the factors which affect our trajectory as a church. Why not go through the Diagnostic questions as a team, discuss the solutions given, and then consider the shifts and tweaks which may need to be made?

HOW TO THOROUGHLY ASSESS YOUR TRAJECTORY AND INTENTIONALLY ACTIVATE FRESH TRACTION IN YOUR CHURCH'S MOMENTUM

10 DIAGNOSTIC QUESTIONS TO ASSESS YOUR MOMENTUM

(Answer 1-10–1 being very poor and 10 being absolutely brilliant—Circle one)

1) How would you rate the level of fullness of your soul right now?

   1   2   3   4   5   6   7   8   9   10

2) How strongly are the mission and vision of your church informing the schedule and activity of you and your team?

   1   2   3   4   5   6   7   8   9   10

3) How effectively is a significant percentage of your church actively mobilized and engaged in reaching new people?

   1   2   3   4   5   6   7   8   9   10

4) How full is the onramp "funnel" of your church with new visitors, guests, and viewers right now?

   1   2   3   4   5   6   7   8   9   10

5) How effective is your current Growth Track at converting at least thirty percent of new identified guests into your small group attenders and/or dream team members?

   1   2   3   4   5   6   7   8   9   10

6) How well is your church connecting and engaging with new visitors and viewers in both the online and in-person spaces?

   1   2   3   4   5   6   7   8   9   10

7) How strongly are your current number and health of your small groups and dream teams positioned to take the church forward right now?

   1   2   3   4   5   6   7   8   9   10

8) How clear and effective is the current development plan for your own leadership?

1   2   3   4   5   6   7   8   9   10

9) How effective is your current Leadership Development Pipeline at intentionally raising three deep leaders across the church?

1   2   3   4   5   6   7   8   9   10

10) How would you rate the current overall momentum trajectory of your church?

1   2   3   4   5   6   7   8   9   10

10 PRACTICAL SOLUTIONS TO CATALYST FRESH MOMENTUM

FULLNESS

1) Leaders operate best out of a reservoir of spiritual overflow and fullness of soul.
2) Leaders do what has to be done to ensure this is their resting state.
3) Blind spots are real, and so leaders need others they trust to keep an eye on this area.

ACTION: Take some time away from the day-to-day to assess and refresh the fullness of your soul and the revival of your Spirit.

ALIGNMENT

1) Many mission and vision statements bear no resemblance to the activities that occur daily.
2) The link between your vision and your tactics is your strategy and systems.
3) Get organized or be content with being a "one person" show.
4) Develop a strategic operating plan that effectively focuses key objectives and allocates resources to maximize the pursuit of the vision.

ACTION: Do a one-day offsite meeting with eight to twelve of your key team to develop a Strategic Operating Plan.

MISSION
1) True disciples are also disciple-makers.
2) One of the key responsibilities of a lead pastor is to mobilize God's people to effectively reach others.
3) This can be measured by the number of identified guests to Sunday services and small groups.

ACTION: The goal is to mobilize thirty to forty percent of your attenders on active mission weekly.

GUESTS
1) New guests are the lifeblood of any church or group.
2) Rolling out the "red carpet" and stewarding them well is one of the greatest opportunities and privileges of every church.
3) Give your VIP team as much focus and attention as your worship team and you'll be well on the way to making this a reality.

ACTION: Shoot for four percent identified guests (i.e., guest cards) of your Sunday attendance.

GROWTH TRACK
1) Almost every church has some sort of Growth Track, but few are doing it well.
2) Clarify the "goalposts" of your Growth Track to get new people engaged in groups first, then teams.
3) Make Growth Track every week a compelling experience of connection, not a content-heavy program.

ACTION: Go for thirty to forty percent of your identified guests to complete Growth Track.

ENGAGEMENT
1) Whilst the church is still talking about "community," the rest of the world is onto vital "connectedness"!

2) Vital connection and engagement with new guests and visitors is your top priority as a church.
3) This can only happen through an intentional strategy and the release of a well-selected and highly-trained VIP team.

ACTION: Develop a highly motivated and skilled VIP team.

SMALL GROUPS

1) The larger a church gets, the smaller it needs to feel, and, in order to get large, the fuel is small groups.
2) Engagement in community and effective discipleship best happens in the context of small groups.

ACTION: Your actual number of small groups should be equal to ten percent of your adult (>sixteen years old) attendance–i.e., 500 ppl in attendance = fifty groups.

CAPACITY

1) You are not the leader you once were, but you are not yet the leader you need to become.
2) This capacity development piece happens accidentally rather than intentionally for way too many leaders.
3) The input of content, benchmarking, and mentoring are essential components in helping you to grow your capacity.

ACTION: Consider getting intentional about dedicating fifteen to thirty minutes per day to ingesting relevant skills-based content, and think seriously about investing in a coach and/or mentor.

PIPELINE

1) Few churches have an "embarrassment of riches" where leaders are concerned.
2) Intentional leadership development involves a combination of culture, content, coaching, and hands-on apprenticeship.

3) It is entirely possible to build a seamless pipeline which will develop disciples and leaders for the current and future needs of the church.

ACTION: Take an objective look at your current Leadership Pipeline, identify any and all the gaps, and then design an effective seamless model.

TRAJECTORY

1) Positive leaders sometimes get caught up in denial if things aren't moving ahead well.
2) Leaders can tend to be addicted to random anecdotes because they are allergic to meaningful empirical data.
3) Brave leaders track everything and are prepared to make both minor adjustments or major shifts according to what is needed.

ACTION: Bravely stand back and assess your current trajectory based on the leading indicators of Identified Guests, Growth Track Completions, Small Group Growth and Reproductions, and Leadership Pipeline Movements.

FUEL YOUR MULTIPLICATION

Discipleship. We hear about its importance, we read about various strategies, and we're sure it's a crucial element to fulfill the mission God has given us, but sometimes we don't integrate it well enough into the fabric of our strategic goals. In this part of our XLR8 Track, we'll see how Empowering Groups and Equipping Leaders can make all the difference.

In many ways, this part of the Momentum Map prepares the church for explosive growth. Some of us assume the Spirit only works spontaneously, but I've found that He is just as active as we craft our *Strategic Plans*, especially in developing leaders.

"And they continued steadfastly in the apostles' doctrine and fellowship, in the breaking of bread, and in prayers. So continuing daily with one accord in the temple, and breaking bread from house to house, they ate their food with gladness and simplicity of heart, praising God and having favor with all the people. And the Lord added to the church daily those who were being saved."

—Acts 2:42, 46-47 (NKJV)

FIFTH GEAR: EMPOWER YOUR GROUPS

It must have been a midlife crisis—that's why I bought a sports car: a black VW EOS convertible.

I had been looking at BMWs, Audis, and Peugeots when my friend suggested I get an EOS. I asked, "A what OS?" I'd never heard of this car, but when I saw it, I loved it! The moment I drove it off the lot, the strangest thing happened: From never having heard of an EOS, there were instantly EOSs everywhere. Had mummy and daddy EOSs all of a sudden started having lots of baby EOSs? Nah, they were obviously there all the time; it was just that I had never noticed them. This is a phenomenon born out of our genius, biological, God-created wiring called the "reticular activating system." It happens to pregnant ladies who, until they're having a baby themselves, seldom notice pregnant women around them, but once they are carrying a child themselves . . . you get the picture.

This phenomenon, as I'm sure you realize, extends far beyond new cars and pregnant women. It applies to the things of God and His mission. When you can imagine copious multiplying small groups whose leaders are genuinely making disciples and intentionally leading each of their group members to take their next step along their faith journey in Christ, you can't unsee it... but beware: sometimes taking the necessary risks to grow groups can get a little messy!

At one point in the earlier days of Hillsong, I was the executive pastor, and Pastor Brian was on a trip to London. Our youth ministry was hitting it out of the park using some creative ways to call young people to a deeper commitment to Christ. The leaders didn't mind making people a little more than a bit uncomfortable because, after all, Jesus told us to pick up our crosses and follow Him. On the way home one day, I was listening to the radio. A news segment reported that a youth group in our area had caused a public nuisance, where police had been called to the scene. As I listened, I shook my head. Maybe a little arrogantly, I thought, here we are, as a church, attempting to build bridges with our community and all these idiots can do is blow them up! The next morning at our staff meeting, I related the story and said how pleased I was that our people hadn't done anything so stupid. After we met, Sam, one of the youth leaders, came over and almost whispered, "Pastor Michael, can I talk to you for a minute?"

"Sure." The look on her face told me trouble was coming.

She began, "You know that story about the youth group on the news?" (I nodded.) "That was us." (We were the idiots!)

I asked her for an explanation, and she told me, "We were trying to make our small groups edgy, so for one of the groups, we had a couple of guys barge in wearing ski masks and kidnap the entire youth small group. They drove them to another location." She took a deep breath and tried to explain the purpose. "We've been talking about the Third World and the persecuted church, and we thought we'd give the small group a taste of what it might be like. It was all in good fun." That last line wasn't very convincing.

She continued, "Everybody in the group got it. They rolled their eyes and said, 'Okay, let's get kidnapped by these terrorists,' but one girl didn't get the joke. When the guys in the masks weren't looking, she ran away and hid behind a bush."

"How did this get on the news?" I asked.

"Well, a lady across the street was looking out her window and saw the girl run and hide. She thought it was a real kidnapping—so did the girl—so she ran outside, grabbed the girl, and brought her inside her home. One of them dialed the emergency number, and within a few minutes, twenty-one squad cars arrived with sirens blaring, guns ready, and the police helicopter hovering overhead."

I spent the day talking to every television network, radio station, and newspaper reporter to explain what had happened.

The moral of the story: Sometimes small groups don't turn out exactly as we planned.

But the logical conclusion shouldn't be that small groups don't work. I sometimes hear from pastors that they've tried small groups, but for some reason, they didn't get traction. "I won't make that mistake again!" they pronounce confidently. I've even heard some Pastors declare "I don't even like small groups!" In my opinion, this is the death knell of true discipleship in their churches. On the other end, some pastors are too easily satisfied with their groups. They look at the number, not the quality and the outcomes. I believe small groups are the only effective and scalable way to consistently make disciples in the local church. I've seen churches count on classes and seminars for their disciple-making. These, though they have been partially effective, in imparting information, fall short of mentoring people in rich, strong relationships that can happen one-on-one, but happen more expansively in small groups.

Take a minute to eavesdrop on a conversation I often have with pastors. I ask, "Pastor, do you have small groups at your church?"

"Oh yes, Michael! We sure do."

"How effective are they?"

"Uh, what do you mean?"

"How many groups do you have?"

"Fifteen."

"Fantastic! If you led one of your neighbors to Christ, and you weren't available to meet regularly with him, so you needed to have someone else disciple him, how many of those groups would you feel completely comfortable and confident handing your neighbor off to?"

Ah, now the wheels are turning. After a few seconds of scanning the groups, he says, "I guess maybe four or five."

"That's okay," I assure him. "That's a lot better than none. But this tells you how many groups are engaging in real discipleship."

I often explain to pastors, "Groups aren't the goal. Discipleship is the goal, and groups are a vehicle to take your church there. Small groups are the smallest scalable unit of disciple-making in the life of the church. You may be the most gifted preacher in your area, but you don't disciple people from the front on Sunday morning. You teach, you inspire, you direct, and you call them to action, but all of these are driven deeper in the give-and-take of small group interactions—or at least, they can be. The God who epitomizes community in the Triune Godhead has created us so that we can thrive only in heart-to-heart connections, which is the beauty and the power of small groups."

The pastor of a church of 500 heard me extol the benefits of small groups, and he asked, "Michael, we have fourteen groups. How can we get more?"

"Great question," I replied. "A good benchmark is to have a group for every ten who attend your church, including adults and children, so in your case, you would shoot for fifty groups." (His eyes widened.) "Your gap is thirty-six groups."

He asked, "That seems . . . really high."

I explained, "These days, most people attend church no more than half the time, and often less, so if you have 500 on a Sunday morning, you actually have 1,000 people who consider themselves to be regular attenders. And if you have people attending only once every three weeks, you have 1,500 people who consider themselves to be part of your church. If 300 of them are children, your pool of potential group members is 1,200. Fifty groups doesn't seem very many for that number of people, does it?"

Actually, I encourage pastors to shoot much higher than one in ten, maybe one in three or four who attend on any given Sunday. Church services generally aren't designed to create and build community. Oh, we ask people to speak to those around them, or in some denominations, we "pass the peace" to one another, but that's hardly "iron sharpening iron" type relationships, right? But in a group, the leader can reinforce what was preached on Sunday and let the message seep into the hearts and change the actions of people in the group. If some of the members aren't very regular in attending Sunday services, the leader can say, "Hey, let's sit together this Sunday and go to lunch after!"

> **Church services generally aren't designed to create and build community.**

What's the purpose of a group? What's the task of the leader? Virtually all of them would say their goal is to create such a life-giving environment that people want to come back. But for many leaders, that's it. "Pastor, I did what you asked. I'm leading a group, and most people like it pretty well." They know they shouldn't teach heresy, and they should provide lots of space for everyone to participate. It's not a platform for Terry the Teacher to exercise his gift.

Let me outline four purposes of a group:

1) CREATE A LIFE-GIVING ENVIRONMENT.

As I mentioned, it is important to create a life-giving environment, to avoid heresy, and to provide space for everyone to participate. That's a good and worthy goal, but it's not the only one.

2) MOVE EVERYONE ONE STEP.

Move everyone to their next step in their journey of spiritual formation. The steps are as varied as the people in the group: trusting in Christ and being born again, being water baptized, being filled with the Spirit, beginning to read the Bible, becoming comfortable with prayer, attending church regularly, serving on a team, sharing their faith, giving generously, finding freedom from emotional and spiritual strongholds, going to counseling for troubling personal or family problems, leading their own group, and so on. Of course, to identify the next step for people in the group, the leaders have to build relationships that are beyond the superficial. If this is a heartfelt goal of leaders, they'll be looking for clues and asking good questions to know their people better as the weeks go by. Many groups are "closed" and "terminal," which means they don't add more people after the group begins, and they plan to meet for a certain number of weeks, maybe eight or ten, and then the group ends. If it went well, the same people may want to sign up for the next series, but those who were too bored or too challenged (and both can be in the same group!) may "vote with their feet" and stop coming after a few weeks. We can ask questions like these:

- "Tell me your God story."
- "Who has been the most positive influence in your spiritual journey?"
- "What's your experience in church?"
- "What is something about faith that you want to explore and become more proficient in?"
- "What's the next step I can help you take?"

We need to avoid telling people what steps they need to take. Self-discovery is a far more powerful motivator. It takes a bit more time, but it's well worth it. (If you perceive that this sounds a lot like personal coaching, you've hit it right on the head. That's exactly the role of a disciple-maker.)

3) BUILD LEADERSHIP THREE DEEP.

We become multiplying disciples when the people in our groups start their own groups. There's nothing revolutionary about that, except that it doesn't happen as often as it could. Leaders should identify a person or a couple who show signs of leadership and begin to equip them to lead a group. I've found that a good debrief after each meeting (or maybe every other meeting) with the prospective new leaders is a great way to give input and get feedback. Yes, I'm well aware that many people hang around after the group meeting is officially over, so you'll need to let people know: "For the next several weeks, we're going to end thirty minutes (or forty-five minutes or whatever works) early because Val and I are going to meet with Sam and Janice to prepare them to lead their own group. The rest of you can continue hanging out next door at Rich and Melissa's house or at the coffee shop, but this is important, so the four of us need this time together." Now, I encourage churches to go beyond identifying and equipping one more set of group leaders. In a group of five or six couples, I tell them to look for two more couples who can be prepared to lead. That way, when the series is over, the next series can begin with three groups instead of one. Some of the people in the original group may go with the new ones, and some will stay. When this after-group coaching begins, there may be others in the group who think, *Huh. I wonder why Michael didn't ask me to lead a group. I think I could do it.* To anticipate that response, I'd announce to the group, "Hey, some others of you may be interested in leading a group. Just let Valery and me know, and we'll be thrilled to talk to you about it."

In the meeting after the meeting, begin by evaluating the meeting you just finished. Ask, "What do you think went well?" And then ask, "What could we have done better?"

After some discussion, be more specific: "Why do you think I asked Jan to share first about Jesus' encouragement about anxiety at the end of Matthew 7?" If they don't know, I'll explain, "Jan always looks on the bright side, so I was pretty sure she would have a faith-filled perspective about our daily worries."

Then I ask, "Why didn't I direct the question to Ronald?"

The couple rolls their eyes and she remarks, "Because Ronald would have talked for the next thirty minutes!"

"Exactly!" Another coaching question: "How did I draw people out?"

The guy realizes that Susan, who seldom speaks, gave her ideas about a particular topic. "Somehow she felt comfortable addressing that issue."

"Did you notice how I asked her?"

"Yeah, you said, 'Susan, you've had a lot of experience with this. Tell us your thoughts about it.' And she did!"

"That's right. Did you see that coming?"

"No, but you obviously did!"

I continue, "Did you see how I handled Dennis' insistence that he was right?"

"Yes, but I don't know if I could handle it that well."

"I've had plenty of time to learn. You just need some tracks to run on. I told him, 'Thanks for giving us your insight, Dennis. Let's you and I talk about it later.' And I moved on quickly to the next question and directed it to someone else in the group. Why did I turn so quickly?"

"So Dennis wouldn't have the chance to demand more time."

"Precisely. See, you're getting it! But that wasn't the end of it. After the group, I met with Dennis in a quiet place. I didn't address the topic he wanted to pontificate on. Instead, I told him as lovingly as I could, 'Dennis, I really value you being in the group, but the group isn't all about you. My job is to give everyone the opportunity to share their thoughts. You understand that, I'm sure."

Coaching is tapping into the other person's insights and motivations. When you find people who want to lead a group, the vast majority of them are sponges soaking up your knowledge, skills, and experience.

(For the after-meeting with the prospective leaders, we recommend a curriculum. Stay tuned for the next chapter.)

4) GET ON MISSION EVERY WEEK.

Group leaders represent the Lord and they represent the church. The pastor relies on these leaders to follow through with the priorities we've addressed in earlier chapters: gaining guests, taking people to Growth Track, sitting in the front at church and taking notes, and actively communicating the grace of God to unbelievers. Groups are the heart and soul of discipleship, and the group leaders are the framework to build a dynamic, soul-winning, disciple-making church. They're not just filling a slot on an organizational chart or providing a holding area for people; the quality of your group leaders determines the effectiveness of your church. Give them the attention the role deserves.

When pastors implement this strategy, they can expect a third of their group leaders to fulfill this vision and launch one or two new groups after the current series. Another third will make an effort, but they won't see multiplication . . . yet. Maybe the timing wasn't right for a couple that would be terrific leaders, or maybe they have all new believers in their group and they need more than a little seasoning. These leaders still have the vision, and the timing will work out sooner or later. And the final third don't even give it a shot.

It's possible, then, to double or even triple the number of groups in the span of one series of eight to ten weeks, but realistically, that's not going to happen. A good rule of thumb is to expect a fifty percent increase, so if you start with fifteen groups, you can expect to have twenty-two or twenty-three for the next series. So here's what I'm saying: Give leaders the aspirational goal of training two couples or individuals. Most of them will identify one and work with them, and half of those will actually start a new group. But hey, a fifty percent increase is fantastic! Do it again and again and again.

Pastor, don't take groups for granted. Don't measure the number of groups; measure their impact. Effective, multiplying, disciple-making groups are the main vehicle to accomplish Jesus's last command to reach everyone on the planet with the life-giving, love-imparting power of the gospel of grace. If you aspire to grow and have a greater impact on your community, this is the strategy that will take you there. The building up and expansion of the body of Christ can only happen in the context of rich relationships, and leaders must provide the environment for them to grow. Then, we'll see in the lives of those in our churches what Paul promised would happen when pastors lead like this:

> *And He Himself gave some to be apostles, some prophets, some evangelists, and some pastors and teachers, for the equipping of the saints for the work of ministry, for the edifying of the body of Christ, till we all come to the unity of the faith and of the knowledge of the Son of God, to a perfect man, to the measure of the stature of the fullness of Christ; that we should no longer be children, tossed to and fro and carried about with every wind of doctrine, by the trickery of men, in the cunning craftiness of deceitful plotting, but, speaking the truth in love, may grow up in all things into Him who is the head—Christ—from whom the whole body, joined and knit together by what every joint supplies, according to the effective working by which every part does its share, causes growth of the body for the edifying of itself in love. —Ephesians 4:11-16*

This is the aspiration and the mandate for discipleship. Don't miss it. XLR8's promise is that a laser focus on getting people into life-changing groups will be the source of God-inspired life-change, personal discipleship for every believer, outward-focused soul-winning, and disciple-making in your church.

Formula 1 teams are always pressing to go faster. They work together, identifying and using the strengths of each person, urging one another to reach a common goal. Pastors, staff members, and group leaders are members of God's pit crew. We need to focus our minds and hearts on the primary goal and stick with it through all the wins and losses.

PIT STOP

To help group members take the next step, leaders can use simple but insightful questions to uncover their hearts' motivations. Here are some I recommend:

1) What's your God story so far?
2) Where would you say you're at right now?
3) How would you describe your relationship with Jesus at the moment? What's going well? What needs shifting?
4) Who have been your two biggest spiritual influences and why?
5) What have you admired about them and what have they most taught/imparted to you?
6) What have been your spiritual highlights to date?
7) How would you describe your spiritual strengths?
8) What have been your spiritual milestones to date?
9) Which areas do you think you may have gotten stuck in?
10) What do you think might be your next discipleship step?
11) Which two of these (show list of possible next steps) would you like to explore?
12) How can I help you move forward in your spiritual journey?

Who are the leaders in your church who really grasp the concept of multiplication?

What do they have that others don't?

How will you implement the four purposes described in this chapter? What do you expect to happen?

"But as for you, continue in what you have learned and have become convinced of, because you know those from whom you learned it, and how from infancy you have known the Holy Scriptures, which are able to make you wise for salvation through faith in Christ Jesus. All Scripture is God-breathed and is useful for teaching, rebuking, correcting and training in righteousness, so that the servant of God a may be thoroughly equipped for every good work."

—2 Timothy 3:14-17

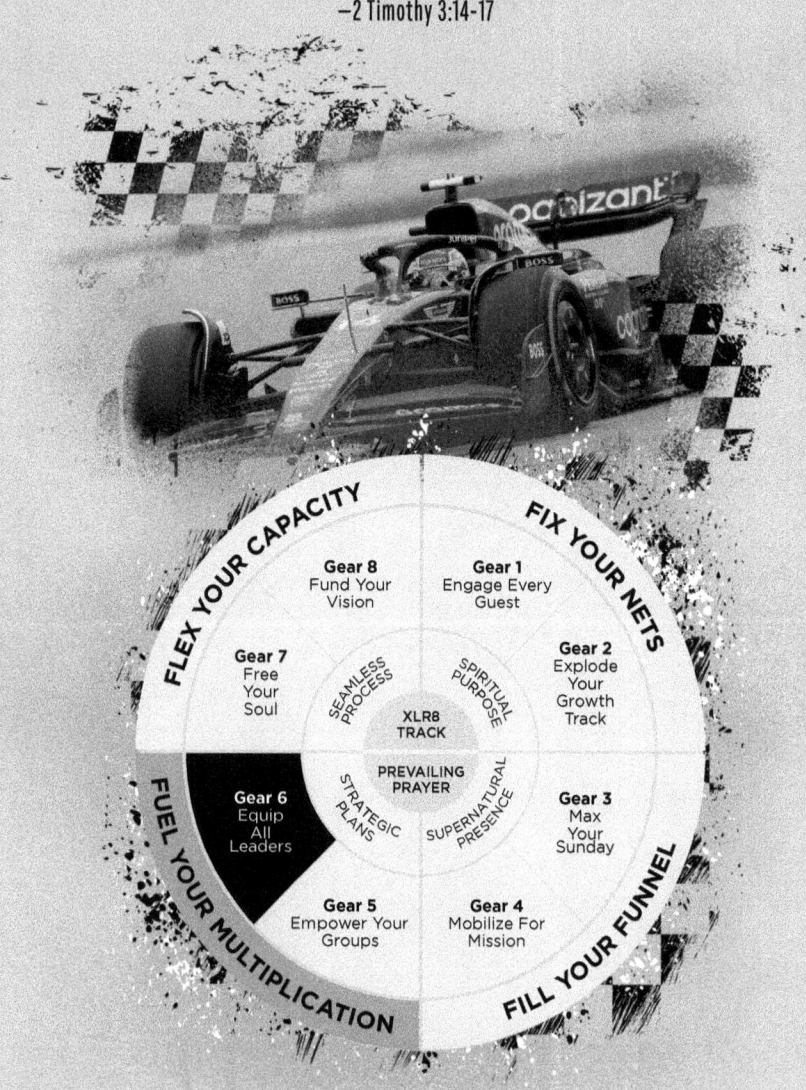

SIXTH GEAR: EQUIP ALL LEADERS

My first company car was a very "special" Mini Minor! It was a rusted-out heap of junk that potentially put my life at risk, but hey, I got to drive it, it was free, and I was nineteen! The most special part about it was the gaping hole in the floor. That's right; there was an actual, literal hole in the floor (four inches or ten centimeters wide) through which you could see the roadway flashing by as you drove along. On one occasion, while attempting to put the "vehicle" in reverse, the gear stick came off in my hand! What the company lacked in their rolling stock of company cars (though the boss did drive a Merc), they made up for in training. Every morning from 7.30 till 9.00, we would all gather for sales training. We covered everything from call scripts to handling objections, to telephone manner, to closing the deal. Over the course of a couple of months, the bunch of ragtag would-be sales guys, mostly in their late teens or early twenties, was turned into a competent group of young sales professionals. Though not everyone made it, it was not for lack of training.

This company, though hardly on the Fortune 500 list, knew something about building an "all hands on deck" approach, and they equipped their teams to succeed... even while driving clapped-out cars.

Far too often, we put people in positions of authority who aren't equipped to carry the weight of responsibility to make disciples. This problem requires a major overhaul. For me, it required a revelation. As a pastor, when I formed my elder board, I chose people who were committed and skilled in leading multiplying groups. As the years went by and we became buddies (mates for my Aussie fam!), I didn't lead them adequately. For a few, the passion and vision for groups eroded bit by bit until we were more of an advisory group than the leaders and examples of multiplying discipleship. They were still elders, and they still had authority, but they weren't as committed to down-and-dirty, in-your-face, grass-roots, compassionate and strong, multiplying discipleship. For months, I was frustrated with them. I believed they had fallen down on their commitments. I tried to avoid letting my anger spill out, but that's like trying to hold ten pounds of trash in a five-pound bag. Then, God showed me that they weren't the problem; I was. Throughout my forty years of ministry, I've tried to always take the position that if there's any tension in a relationship, I want to take the initiative to apologize. Almost without fail, this gesture opens the door of communication, defensiveness subsides, and understanding begins. Many years ago, when I was on the staff at a church, the senior pastor, who had become a trusted friend, began treating me in a way that was less than our relationship deserved. After this went on for a week, I walked into his office, knelt on the floor, and said, "Pastor, tell me what I've done that has upset you so much."

He tried to shake me off like nothing was wrong, but I pressed ahead: "Something has changed. You're frustrated with me. Let me say upfront, whatever I've done—and I hope you'll tell me specifically—I want to tell you I'm deeply sorry. The last thing I want is to do something that harms our relationship because our relationship is very important to me."

He put his head down and whispered, "Michael, it's not you. It's me. I'm working through some stuff, and obviously, it has spilled out on you."

I responded, "Thank you for telling me. What can I do to help you?" In those few moments, the tension was resolved, compassion reigned, and a friendship was restored.

Years later, I knew I needed to apply this lesson with my eight elders. When the Lord showed me that I had fallen down in my leadership, I met with them in our boardroom at Shire Live and announced, "Gentlemen, I need to make a confession."

That got their attention. They weren't sure what was coming. I assured them, "No, no, nothing like what you're thinking. It's about my leadership." I let that sink in, and then I continued, "We're good friends, and I really treasure our friendships. I'm so grateful to God for you, but somewhere along the way, I stopped being your pastor. I apologize. I don't want to stop being your friend, but I need to recalibrate our relationship so I don't avoid my responsibility of being your pastor and draw the God-greatness in your walks with Him. It's my responsibility to encourage you, yes, but also to challenge you to live, love, and serve at your highest capacity. I realized that I've allowed our friendship to eclipse my leadership responsibility. I ask you to forgive me."

With my preemptive apology, their hearts became responsive to my confession. Several of them said things like, "No, Pastor Michael, it's not you; it's me. I've been preoccupied with problems at work, and you know what's going on with my teenage daughter. I've dropped the ball. If anyone should apologize, it's me."

I told them, "I appreciate your willingness to take responsibility too. That means a lot to me, but we need to recalibrate our relationships. Will we still be friends? Absolutely. Will we still all go out to dinner together with our spouses? Certainly. Am I going to step up to be the voice of Christ in your lives the way God wants me to? Yes, and I'll tell you, there may be some uncomfortable conversations . . . ones we should have had months ago. For instance, it wasn't that long ago that we were all leading small groups, and all of us were intentional about mentoring couples or individuals in our groups to become leaders. I know you've been busy, and I know you've been under pressure at work, and for some of you, at home. I get all that, but from today, we're moving in a direction so that all of us exemplify the things we say are vitally important. We need to do what we're preaching and asking others to do. In the next month or so, I want you to get back into the groove to gather people and lead a small group, and I want you to ask God to give you at least one couple or person who will start leading a group when yours ends. I'll be glad to help. If you have a problem with this, if this isn't where your heart is, or if the burdens you carry are too great at this time, we'll talk about it privately." This conversation was a massive breakthrough . . . for me and for them.

When we think of leadership training, we often move immediately to tactics and miss the fundamental truth that is the heart and soul of good and godly leadership: the identity, gifting, and calling of every believer. As I've mentioned, we're not setting up a meeting for a social club, and we're not just hanging out with people. Believers "have been bought with a price," and God considers us His "treasures." We are indwelled by the Spirit of God, given the most noble calling the world has ever known. In The Call, Professor Os Guinness explains the enormous scope of God's hand on us: "Calling is the truth that God calls us to himself so decisively that everything we are, everything we do, and everything we have is invested with a special devotion and dynamism lived out as a response to his summons and service."[7] Including leading worship, preaching, caring for the poor and orphans, feeding the hungry . . . and leading small groups. When we train group leaders, we're equipping them to have a profound impact on individuals, families, communities, and the world. Are specific tactics in leading people important? Of course, but we need to know whose we are before we tackle what we do.

> When we train group leaders, we're equipping them to have a profound impact on individuals, families, communities, and the world.

I've heard pastors claim, "We don't use any kind of organized plan to train our group leaders. We do it organically." And I respond, "Good luck with that!" If we want to scale up our group leadership and participation, we need a structure that imparts wisdom and skills. I've met with plenty of men and women who told me, "Pastor, I really want to disciple people so they grow in their faith, but I just don't know how. Would you help me?" That's what a leadership training structure is all about, equipping the saints for ministry.

Some churches have a quarterly group leaders' meeting where the pastor brings an inspiring message, dinner is served, people enjoy one another, and they go home saying, "I love this church!" There's nothing wrong with that, but it's not enough. The leaders haven't been equipped with specific skills and tools to lead more effectively.

---

7 Os Guinness, *The Call* (Nashville: Thomas Nelson, 2003), p. 5.

Other churches hold the same kind of meeting, but before dinner, they break out into groups to address specific tactics of group leadership, and they may meet according to the kinds of groups they lead: couples, men, women, youth, ex-cons, etc. This may be a good refresher for those who have developed skills over years of leading, but it's not enough for new leaders.

Corporations leave nothing to chance. They have regular and detailed training programs for all their employees, and at the higher levels, professional development is one of the highest priorities—the success of the company depends on it. When I was in corporate sales before I became a pastor, our company had three days of intensive training three times a year. They taught us the principles, modeled them in action, gave us opportunities to practice them, and then gave us feedback so we could improve. This is the concept churches need to emulate in training group leaders. Let me list and then describe a dozen specific skills leaders need to acquire:

LIFE GROUP LEADER TRAINING TOPICS

1) Creating a great group atmosphere.
2) Catalyzing group-centric growth.
3) Connecting people together.
4) Curating spiritual potency.
5) Encouraging group engagement.
6) Managing group dynamics.
7) Handling difficult people.
8) Triaging life crises.
9) Helping everyone take their next discipleship step.
10) Uncovering people's calling.
11) Mobilizing all members on mission.
12) Raising your future leaders.

1) CREATING A GREAT GROUP ATMOSPHERE.

People are moved and come back for more—to church, a group, a game, a club, or any other event—because of what they felt, not the information downloaded into their brains. It's vital for group leaders to assess the environment of the room: the lighting, the temperature, the seating arrangement, the refreshments, and everything else that stimulates meaningful interaction. Some leaders intuitively grasp this concept, but others need a checklist. The leader is, as a friend suggested, "the director of ambiance." My friend Rod Plummer leads a church of over 3,000 people in Japan. The people who attend have relatively small homes, so many of their groups are held in coffee shops or at the church on Sundays. Again, we become aware of all five senses. If people feel uncomfortable or disconnected, they won't feel loved and valued . . . and they may not come back to give the leader a second chance. An important part of creating an engaging atmosphere is welcoming people warmly. Who is at the front door? How are people greeted, especially in the first couple of weeks of the group? And during the meeting, what's the interpersonal atmosphere? Is there unspoken tension? Are people bored or confused? Is Talkative Tina sucking all the air out of the room? Or is there a warm, affirming environment where no question is out of line, even if it may not be answered during the meeting? I'll repeat it again: The questions people are thinking but not asking are, "Do these people like me?" and "Do I like them?" Answer these questions with warmth, and you'll be off to a great start.

2) CATALYZING GROUP-CENTRIC GROWTH.

One of the most common comments from new group leaders sounds like this: "Pastor, I'm ready to start my group, but you haven't sent any people to me." We need to shift the responsibility for invitations from the pastor to the leaders. Every leader has a sphere of influence. Within that sphere, leaders can expect perhaps one in three personal invitations to be accepted. If the leader receives a list of people who indicated on a guest card that they want to be in a group, the number is almost certainly even higher. So, if a leader wants to have ten people in the new group, he needs to invite twenty-five to thirty people. During the eight- to ten-week series, the one or two individuals or couples who want to start groups can be tapping people to join them when the next group begins, and the current leader can tap some to take their place as new leaders (if the group stays together and continues).

3) CONNECTING PEOPLE TOGETHER.

The goal is to create such a positive atmosphere that every person says something in every meeting—and every comment receives affirmation: "Thank you, Janice. That was a very interesting insight." "Great question, Jack." "You have really studied this, Rhonda!" "Bob, tell us more about that." The people being trained to lead new groups need to see themselves as vital contributors to this culture of affirmation. The kind words, though, must be genuine, not over the top, or you'll degrade the warmth you're trying to create.

4) CURATING SPIRITUAL POTENCY.

I'm talking about real potency... without being weird. We believe the Spirit of God is working powerfully in the lives of people today, and we expect to see the impact of His presence. We pray and expect God to work wonders of healing, guidance, repentance, and reconciliation. If someone tries to go over the top and begins to freak people out, calmly explain that there's nothing strange about believing God to intervene in powerful ways. New leaders may have faith to believe

God to cure a headache, but they want to call in the big guns on the pastoral staff for a cancer diagnosis. Part of the training is to explain to people that we belong to a kingdom of royal priests, and all of us can go to the throne of grace to plead for God's mercy and power to be revealed in the lives of those we love. When I led my first group, after being a Christian for about a year, I fasted and prayed all day before our group met. I wanted God to protect our people from any heresy that might come out of my mouth, and I wanted God to move in power in their lives. And He did. Over the next couple of years, our group multiplied through seven generations. I didn't know any better. I thought it was normal.

5) MANAGING GROUP DYNAMICS.

This is how potency is expressed in a group. I used to joke that when people came to our group, within a couple of months, they were all bald because we laid hands on them so often when we prayed! Every leader creates a sense of normalcy by instituting habits such as humor, appropriate vulnerability, and pleasant banter. The variety is wide, but the elements need to include genuine trust in the presence, pardon, and power of God to change lives. The group isn't the place to try to resolve the most difficult theological issues of history, and casting out demons probably shouldn't be the go-to solution for every person's problem. If someone leans too hard into things like this, take it offline to have a personal conversation about the purpose of the group and the atmosphere you're trying to create.

6) HANDLING DIFFICULT PEOPLE.

I love to talk about this with group leaders because they instantly think of people they've had in their group. One leader told me, "My wife leads a women's group, and she had a lady who wouldn't stop talking. She said she tried every strategy she'd ever learned—not giving eye contact, redirecting the conversation, interrupting with a 'thank you' and pressing on—but nothing worked. Then she told me, 'She's going to your recovery group tonight.' I told her, 'I'll handle it. No problem.' That night in my group, that lady started talking and didn't take a breath for a long time. I pulled out every technique I'd ever learned, but nothing worked. Finally, I had to say, 'Joanne, you really need to stop talking now!' When I got home, my wife asked how it had gone with Joanne. I didn't want to tell her!" The most common types of difficult people include those who talk too much, "toxic sharers" who tell far too much, the person who never talks, the one who has all the right answers, the sullen person who never has anything positive to say, and the couple who arrive just after a big fight and their seething anger pervades the room. Leaders can learn to address some of these in the group with grace and set boundaries so no one dominates the conversation, and talk to some of them after the group.

7) TRIAGING LIFE CRISES.

You don't get a second chance to take a bite of the cherry. When someone in the group faces a crisis, show up, shut up, and put on the kettle. Show up—just being there means the world to people who are hurting. Shut up—they may need some insight a month later, but not today, not now, and not you. (See "Show up.") Put on the kettle— bring a meal, some flowers, or a couple of magazines if the person will be in the hospital waiting room for long periods. Put yourself in that person's shoes and do for them what you'd like someone to do for you. In widespread disasters like hurricanes, earthquakes, and fires, leaders have to triage their involvement: Who needs help now, and who can wait a bit? Who else can jump in to provide care? What resources can be brought to bear?

8) DEVELOPING A CULTURE OF GENUINE CARE.

Paul wrote to the Colossians to describe how the gospel of grace transforms us in our relationships: "Therefore, as the elect of God, holy and beloved, put on tender mercies, kindness, humility, meekness, longsuffering; bearing with one another, and forgiving one another, if anyone has a complaint against another; even as Christ forgave you, so you also must do. But above all these things put on love, which is the bond of perfection" (Colossians 3:12-14). This is how we treat them, and this is how we pray for them. As our hearts are increasingly entwined with theirs, we take them and their concerns to God, perhaps daily, but certainly regularly.

9) HELPING EVERYONE TAKE THEIR NEXT DISCIPLESHIP STEP.

We've already addressed this, but it doesn't hurt to remind you that one of the primary goals of a group leader is helping each person take the next step in their faith journey. It may be internal, perhaps getting free of bondage to shame or being healed from the wounds of abuse; it may be external, like a physical illness; it may be relational, like a strained connection with a family member or friend; or it could be in their career, like relating to a difficult boss or a career opportunity. If you don't know what the step is, you can't help them take it.

10) UNCOVERING PEOPLE'S CALLINGS.

We need to learn to see people through Jesus' eyes. As I mentioned earlier in this chapter, God has put a rich calling on the life of all believers, no matter how publicly acclaimed or obscure they may be.

When we think of the Reformation in the sixteenth century, we usually focus on Luther's emphasis on grace instead of works as the basis of our salvation, but there's another important feature of Luther's teaching: the priesthood of all believers. When leaders see every person in the group as one who is a royal priest, it revolutionizes their perspective, raises their expectations, and energizes conversations. The leader's goal is to look for keys in each person to unlock their God-given potential and motivation to make a difference.

11) MOBILIZING ALL MEMBERS ON MISSION.

It's important for people throughout the church to be mobilized in bringing people to church and to faith in Christ, and groups are the environment where this strategy takes deeper root. Leaders need to make it a priority to pray for the lost, especially the specific people who are in the top three of those in the group.

12) RAISING YOUR FUTURE LEADERS.

We shouldn't make too many assumptions about those being mentored to become group leaders in the next cycle. The training program should address the important topics of "the meeting after the meeting" to debrief, widening the pool of people to invite, how to invite them, and how to get off to a banging start when the group begins.

The excellence and heart of the pastor's efforts to equip small group leaders determine the breadth and depth of disciple-making and multiplication in the church. Don't take it for granted. Give it everything you've got.

The goal is not just having a group! XLR8's promise is that outstanding training of group leaders will change the landscape of your church, but it doesn't happen without a clear vision and determined effort to equip leaders—new ones and veterans—to be their best.

These people will become your catalysts for change, moving people to their next step of spiritual growth . . . and the next . . . and the next.

Engineers and mechanics who work on Formula 1 cars are astute observers of what works and what doesn't, and they hone their craft so the car can be at its very best. That's the example for us as we train the people who are the hands-on disciple-makers in our churches.

PIT STOP: POTENTIAL NEXT STEPS FOR . . .

ME
1) Connect
2) Salvation
3) Water Baptism
4) Word
5) Prayer
6) Spirit Baptism
7) Freedom

US
1) Church
2) Group
3) Serving
4) Giving
5) Discipling
6) Family
7) Equipped

THEM
1) Witness
2) Assistant Leader
3) Group Leader

4) Development Plan
5) Group Coach
6) Calling
7) Mission

QUESTIONS TO HELP PEOPLE TAKE THE NEXT STEP
1) What's your God story so far?
2) Where would you say you're at right now?
3) How would you describe your relationship with Jesus at the moment? What's going well? What needs shifting?
4) Who have been your two biggest spiritual influences and why?
5) What have you admired about them and what have they most taught/imparted to you?
6) What have been your spiritual highlights to date?
7) How would you describe your spiritual strengths?
8) What have been your spiritual milestones to date?
9) Which areas do you think you may have gotten stuck in?
10) What do you think might be your next discipleship step?
11) Which two of these (show list of possible next steps) would you like to explore?
12) How can I help you move forward in your spiritual journey?

FLEX YOUR CAPACITY

Far too many pastors are burdened by past wounds and mistakes, and their church's growth is limited by a lack of resources. In these chapters, we'll look at solutions to both of these common problems.

Leading a church is one of the most stressful careers in the world. Many have compared it to "herding cats." To lead well, pastors need to avoid (as much as possible) the conflicting purposes of pleasing God and avoiding the criticism of people. The only way to do that is to have our hearts rooted in the limitless love, forgiveness, and power of God. As our souls are increasingly free to serve God wholeheartedly, we can experience the *Seamless Process* of acquiring and utilizing every resource for His honor.

"For though we walk in the flesh, we do not war according to the flesh. For the weapons of our warfare are not carnal but mighty in God for pulling down strongholds, casting down arguments and every high thing that exalts itself against the knowledge of God, bringing every thought into captivity to the obedience of Christ."

—2 Corinthians 10:3-5

SEVENTH GEAR: FREE YOUR SOUL

I got behind the wheel of a car for the first time when I was fourteen. A man from our local church invited three of us to take a spin with him in his speedboat. The other two guys backed out at the last minute, so it was just the man and me. It felt 'off' somehow. I rode with him as we towed the boat. He carefully backed the trailer down the ramp and tied the boat off at the dock. He drove the car and trailer to the parking lot. We got in the boat, and he opened it up as soon as we were away from the no-wake zone. After a few disturbing hours on the bay, it was time to go home. As he approached the dock, the current was flowing fast, and he had difficulty lining the boat up with the trailer. He asked me to get out of the boat and sit in the driver's seat in the car. Then he yelled for me to back slowly down the ramp until the trailer was deep enough in the water. I thought, *How hard could this be?* But instead of letting gravity take the car down the ramp, I took my foot off the brake, put it in reverse, and hit the accelerator! A couple of seconds later, the car was submerged to the windows. Oooops!

We sat for what seemed like hours until a tow truck arrived to drag us—the car, the boat, and the trailer—out of the water and up to the parking lot. It was an excruciating time, not so much because of the guilt I felt for ruining the guy's car, but because I had to spend all that time with someone who had just sexually molested me when we were alone out in the middle of the bay. (More about this later.)

Years later when I trusted in Jesus, I was gloriously saved, but I was still terribly insecure. I lived by the smiles or frowns of the people around me, and I learned to read them like a book! When I was at Hillsong, I was quickly elevated to a leadership role because of my charisma and gifts, but I moved into a role that was beyond my spiritual maturity. I tried desperately to cover up my insecurities with outstanding performance. In the heady days of our youth revival, I was so busy *doing* that I didn't think much about *being*. In the adrenaline rush of accomplishing something for God, it was easy to miss the motivation of my doing coming out of being God's loved, forgiven, accepted child. At times, my soul was as dry as an old boot, and I was, as the Jackson Browne song goes, "Running on empty, running blind, running into the sun, but I'm running behind."[8]

> In the heady days of our youth revival, I was so busy *doing* that I didn't think much about *being*.

We scheduled Chuck Girrard, an American Christian Gospel singer to come for a concert, and the room was packed. It looked like a billion people crammed into the space. (It was probably about 800.) A number of kids got saved, and the whole thing was a big success. After it was over, I hung around to help the band pack up. A couple, Philip

---
8 Jackson Browne, "Running on Empty," *Running on Empty* Album, 1978.

and Marcia, had both been addicts before they met Christ. Their lifestyle, though, had taken a toll on them: they looked like they'd lived many more hard years than their twenty-odd-years lives. I'd seen them many times over the previous months, and we always had very pleasant, if brief, chats. They were always so excited that they had found Jesus, and they talked about what He was doing in their lives. I expected the same thing this time, so I asked enthusiastically, "Hey, how are the two of you doing?"

She looked away and nodded, "Okay, I guess."

He stared at me and said, "Pastor Michael, I think God has left me."

I went into a different mode: "Philip, talk to me. What's going on?"

"I . . . I just don't feel God anymore. Something's wrong."

I put my hand on his shoulder and told him, "Philip, this is a great sign."

He was shocked. "How can that be?"

I explained, "In the early days of your experience with Jesus, He confirmed your relationship with Him by quick responses to your prayers and feeling close—and that was wonderful. Now, to help you grow in your faith—so that your relationship with Him is based more on faith and not just feelings—He sometimes delays answers to prayer and withholds some of the warm feelings. He wants you to trust in His Word, not in your emotions at any given moment. We are to trust in God's truth no matter how we feel, but as we speak out the truth of God, His Word often reactivates that sense of closeness—maybe not instantly, but sooner or later."

As I spoke these words to Philip, the Holy Spirit whispered, "And what about you, Buck-o?"

I felt that my heart had been struck a blow, and I knew I had to recalibrate my relationship with God. That week, I took a train (something I seldom did) from Rockdale Station. As I stood on the platform before the train arrived, people were milling around. It was a very normal day at the station, but suddenly, I thought about my conversation with Philip, and the Lord brought a simple verse to mind: "The joy of the Lord is your strength." I said it out loud, and said it again. And again and again. In that moment, I felt the rush of the presence of God. I'm surprised no one tapped me on the shoulder and said, "Hey, dude, where can I buy what you're on?"

While I was at Hillsong, Pastor Brian's approval was really important to me . . . and I deeply felt it when it wasn't there—or worse, criticized anything I was doing. His affirmation meant far too much to me. Rather than being a statement about him, this was about me. One time when I was on holiday, a thought plagued me that he was going to replace me. I envisioned him taking my name off the door of my office and putting someone else's name there. This image became a powerful stronghold in my mind and heart. I was supposed to be relaxing and recharging, but I was consumed with the fear of failure and rejection. I didn't tell Valery. It was my own private battle that week . . . and I was losing it.

I hate to say it, but this wasn't a temporary problem. For my first fifteen years in ministry, I often had unrest in my soul. Some people might offer some advice, "Why didn't you pray?" Oh, I prayed. I often prayed for two or three hours at night after Valery and I put the kids to bed. I always had a place, my prayer closet, in our little home. Or I went to a hill in the pitch-black night to beat on the doors of heaven. I had a Palm Pilot (remember those?) with a stylus, and I jotted down my thoughts on the lit-up screen.

I regularly went into "God's dream theater" in my prayers. I prayed in the Spirit, and as often happens, the first few minutes were full of distractions, but after a while, the distractions were washed away in the presence of God. It was like being in a theater watching a movie. It wasn't always visions and pictures, but there were often words and impressions that brought joy to my heart. These were precious times when God imparted wisdom, power, and love, but when my prayers were over, I went back to being a hugely flawed, shame-driven, clay-footed, broken man. (No wonder I prayed so much!)

Where did all that shame, fear, and insecurity come from? When I grew up, I was the oldest son of seven kids. Mum was so loving and affirming. Dad was an incredible provider, sometimes working three jobs: a funeral director, an emcee at a Talent Quest on Friday nights, and pulling beers at the local football club on Saturday nights. Almost every Sunday morning, Dad came home with a box of Rose's Chocolates. All nine of us were in Mum and Dad's bed rummaging through the box, looking for the prized pieces of candy—the hard ones.

Back to the story at the opening of this chapter: I was a young, growing fourteen-year-old when I went for the boat ride with the man who had been attending our local church. I sometimes played tennis with him and a couple of guys who were a bit older than me. I was the young kid, and I proudly wore the honor of acceptance into their group. When the other two backed out of his invitation to go for a ride in his boat, it was just him and me. We sped around the bay for a long time. It was exhilarating! When we were far from shore, he turned off the engine and told me he had really been helped by getting massages for his aching muscles. He knew I was playing football (Aussie Rules for my Americans friends) at the time, and he asked, "Do you have any pains?"

I told him I had a few, so he offered, "Would you like me to give those places a rubdown? It'll feel a lot better."

I was clueless, so I said, "Sure."

Gradually, his hands moved over my body to parts that weren't sore at all. It was my first sexual experience, and it was terribly confusing. It was wrong and horrible, but it felt good. I wondered, *Am I gay? Did*

I ask for it somehow? Why did he pick me? I wrestled with all kinds of fear and doubts, and I became determined to show that I wasn't gay by sleeping with as many girls as I could.

My promiscuous behavior resulted in a girlfriend's pregnancy—she was the daughter of the leading Catholic family with nine kids in a neighboring parish. I remember talking to her dad to inform him that I had made his precious daughter pregnant. It didn't go well. In those days, unwed pregnancies were far more of a stigma than today, especially for the high-profile Catholic parents of the girl. We were both eighteen and planned to get married. I gave her my grandmother's engagement ring. I dropped out of my commerce law degree at university and got three jobs to earn some money to set up house for my soon-to-be bride and our almost-as-soon-to-be child. I saved about $12,000. The relationship, however, fell apart. Her parents wanted her to get as far away from me as possible, and to be honest, I don't blame them. (Honestly, I would have done exactly the same thing if I were them!) I was an irresponsible young man who was full of himself—not the kind of son-in-law they'd been looking for.

When she told me she wasn't going to marry me, I sobbed like a baby. But I quickly realized I had all this money in my hands (and at the time, that amount seemed like a million dollars). I decided to numb the pain any way I could. I got into some trouble in King's Cross, the city's red light district. I made friends with some of the local police, so they invited me to join them after their shifts when they went into the back rooms where their special clients enjoyed food and drink and relaxed.

There were several times when I could have lost my life. I've described one of those when I was driving way too fast while I was stone-drunk. I lost control and turned the car over. I was banged up, but it could have been much worse.

By that time, I was at the end of my rope. That's when I wandered into the service where Brian Houston was preaching. I heard the gospel of grace, and I went forward to receive Christ as my Savior and Lord. I finally found meaning, peace, and joy—what I'd been missing since that day on the water when I was fourteen. But the internal damage didn't magically vanish that day. My spirit came alive, but my soul was as broken as ever. After the first blush of relief and gratitude ebbed, I was still wracked with fear, shame, doubt, and insecurity. My soul was still in bondage, and I needed to be set free.

The truth of the gospel, applied to our deepest wounds and highest hopes, sets us free, but we need to know how to apply it. Paul used a shorthand expression "in Christ" or "in Him" to pack a huge amount of truth. We are "in Christ" in the crucifixion, so when He died, our sins were paid for. We are "in Him" in His sinless life, so His perfect life is credited to us as righteousness. We are "in Him" in the resurrection, so we have a new kind of life that is based on and empowered by the same power that raised Jesus from the tomb. And we are "in Him" in the ascension, so as Jesus sits at the right hand of God, we have spiritual authority delegated to us. That's theology; let me put it in a narrative. When Jesus came to His cousin John at the Jordan, He was baptized—not because He needed to repent from sin, but because He wanted to identify Himself with sinners. Matthew takes us to the river: "When He had been baptized, Jesus came up immediately from the water; and behold, the heavens were opened to Him, and He saw the Spirit of God descending like a dove and alighting upon Him. And suddenly a voice came from heaven, saying, 'This is My beloved Son, in whom I am well pleased'" (Matthew 3:16-17). We see the Trinity in action, and three important truths are illustrated here: *identity*—"This is My Son"; *acceptance*—"My beloved Son"; and *approval*—"in whom I am well pleased." If we are "in Christ," the Father bestows these three blessings on us, just as He did for Jesus. We don't earn them; they're a free gift. Jesus's identity as the Father's child becomes our identity, His acceptance becomes ours, and the Father's approval of Jesus is showered on us.

These blessings come first and foremost from God, but also from the family of God. We need people who affirm our identity, model God's acceptance, and display their approval. And notice: these things were said to Jesus before He performed any miracles, preached any messages, told any parables, or did anything in His ministry. Identity, acceptance, and approval precede performance.

The signs of insecurity are many and varied, and in fact, can take opposite tacks. For instance:

- Never having an opinion . . . or being dogmatic and insisting you're right about everything.
- Having racing, uncontrolled negative thoughts . . . or being so mentally and emotionally numb that you can't think.
- Living with a chronic inability to make decisions . . . or making impulsive, rash decisions.
- Reliving conversations over and over as a kind of self-punishment . . . or remaining oblivious to the impact of conversations.
- Insisting on your way for any decision or project . . . or letting others make all the decisions.
- Frequently putting people down so you'll look good . . . or bestowing elaborate and effusive praise to earn approval.
- Trying to impress people by boasting . . . or trying to hide from any chance of negative feedback.
- Being hyper-sensitive to criticism . . . or developing such a thick skin that nothing can get through.

- Glaring, being loud, and demanding your way . . . or trying to evaporate into thin air because you can't stand even disagreement, much less conflict.

We can probably identify plenty of others, but you get the idea.

Insecure pastors and other leaders must find something to give them an identity, acceptance, and approval if they don't drink deeply of the grace of God. Like me for those fifteen years, they reach for counterfeits, behaviors, and status that promise security, and they deliver for a moment but leave them feeling even more desperate. I call these false hopes "traps" because they snare us like a bear trap. We can easily identify a number of these: being seen as better than others, being awarded status based on our performance, demanding to be in control of situations and the people around us, and expecting people to treat us like royalty. And I'm not just talking about megachurch pastors. Even pastors of small churches can act like they're kings of their fiefdoms. These traps are idols. It's fascinating that John ends his first letter with this warning: "Little children, keep yourselves from idols. Amen" (1 John 5:21). If you look back through the letter, he hasn't mentioned idols a single time . . . or maybe, just maybe, the whole letter has been a warning about making power, prestige, and possessions more important to our souls than Jesus.

In his commencement address at Kenyon College, novelist David Foster Wallace told the graduates who were about to embark on their great quest for meaning:

> *"If you worship money and things—if they are where you tap real meaning in life—then you will never have enough. Never feel you have enough. It's the truth. Worship your own body and beauty and sexual allure and you will always feel ugly, and when time and age start showing, you will die a million deaths before they finally plant you. On one level, we all know*

> this stuff already—it's been codified as myths, proverbs, clichés, bromides, epigrams, parables: the skeleton of every great story. The trick is keeping the truth up front in daily consciousness. Worship power—you will feel weak and afraid, and you will need ever more power over others to keep the fear at bay. Worship your intellect, being seen as smart—you will end up feeling stupid, a fraud, always on the verge of being found out."[9]

Idols, false gods, traps, counterfeits... whatever you want to call them enslave us because we keep going back again and again under the spell that this time they'll give us what we want, but they starve us because they can only provide temporary relief—they leave us feeling empty and desperate for more.

Adultery is a good example. In most cases, it doesn't start out about sex. It's either the longing to be known and loved, or it's the bragging rights that you conquered this person, or the sheer power of being able to get what you want. The first one at least values the other person to some extent; the other two are entirely self-centered.

When we seek identity, approval, and acceptance in something other than God, our souls deteriorate, but we cling to those things because we believe their promises. God speaks directly to the attractive but deceiving counterfeits through Jeremiah:

> "Thus says the LORD:
> "Let not the wise man glory in his wisdom,
> Let not the mighty man glory in his might,
> Nor let the rich man glory in his riches;
> But let him who glories glory in this,
> That he understands and knows Me,

---

[9] David Foster Wallace, "This Is Water," Kenyon College, www.theguardian.com/books/2008/sep/20/fiction

> *That I am the* LORD, *exercising lovingkindness, judgment, and righteousness in the earth.*
> *For in these I delight," says the* LORD.
> —Jeremiah 9:23-24

Only Jesus can fill the gaping hole in our hearts. Only Jesus can satisfy our deepest longing. Only Jesus can tell us who we are and where we belong. But we've heard this for years, haven't we? Why is it so hard to really believe it? A little later in Jeremiah, the prophet tells us the problem: "The heart is deceitful above all things, and desperately wicked: who can know it?" (vs. 17:9)

Jesus told the religious leaders of His day, "You are of your father the devil, and the desires of your father you want to do. He was a murderer from the beginning, and does not stand in the truth, because there is no truth in him. When he speaks a lie, he speaks from his own resources, for he is a liar and the father of it" (John 8:44). And Paul reminds the Romans that the enemy has always used lies to deceive, discourage, and disempower: "Therefore God also gave them up to uncleanness, in the lusts of their hearts, to dishonor their bodies among themselves, who exchanged the truth of God for the lie, and worshiped and served the creature rather than the Creator, who is blessed forever. Amen" (Romans 1:24-25).

The problem Paul described wasn't just the end results, the sinful behavior; the real problem is the mindset, their thinking, and believing. People who pursue counterfeits (and news flash, we all do to one degree or another while we're in this life) need a checkup from the neck up. If we can summon even a morsel of humility and honesty about what goes on in our minds, we have an early warning system so we can keep our hearts riveted on Jesus, the only true source of security and meaning. One leader observed that our real god is what we think about when we have nothing else to think about—it's what has captured our hearts and fills our minds with desire and fear—the desire to get it and the fear of losing it. For instance, if the musing of your unpressured heart is about sexual exploits, either in person or online, sit up and notice. And if someone touches your arm and it sets off urges, that's a warning signal. In many ways, this is just a part of being human, but Christian leaders are called to a higher standard. We must tell someone what's going on with us. We must have a coach, counselor, or friend who can hear the worst about us and not run away, laugh, or ridicule. I heard Pastor Chris Hodges say, "If you've got secrets no one knows about, you're already in trouble."

Before I joined the staff of Hillsong, I was a medical rep, and I traveled quite a bit. On one of my trips, I checked into a hotel where a number of others in sales were staying. As I received my key, another rep, a very attractive young woman, walked up to the counter to check-in. I noticed. When I got to my room, my years of sexual encounters flooded my mind, and I thought about making it with this woman. I was newly married, so instead of hiding my lust from Valery, I called her to ask for her support. She talked me down, and I came back to sanity. But this pretty woman's room was next to mine, and she brought a guy to her room for the night. The walls were paper thin, and I was in purgatory all night. I thought, That could have been me! Earlier in the night, that thought would have brought disappointment, but now it made me really thankful.

Later, I was promoted to project manager in marketing for Pfizer. Once a quarter, we traveled to deliver the new marketing strategy and materials to the reps around the country. We stayed at posh hotels and held nice dinners. One night in Adelaide, my boss invited the rest of us on the team to go out. I had just finished going over my PowerPoint presentation for the next day, and I was tired. I hesitated, but he said, "Come on, Michael. Just get in the taxi. We'll have some fun." After the drive, we pulled up to a building on Hindley Street, and I noticed there were no windows. As soon as we walked in, I saw that the girls had on see-through blouses. I was a new Christian with hypersensitivity to seductive women, so I sat with my head down and my back toward the girls. I caught my boss's eye. He was watching to see how I'd react. One of the girls came over—and leaned over—to ask, "Can I get you a drink?"

I stammered, "Uh, yes, a Coke, please."

I kept telling myself, I've got to get out of here! And a minute later, I had a plan. I asked everyone within earshot, "Does anyone have a taxi voucher?"

My boss asked, "Why do you need one, Michael?"

"I just need to go." That was the sum total of my answer.

I got a taxi back to the hotel and went straight to my room. I turned on the television and found a test match between two cricket teams, and I called Valery. I told her what happened, and I explained, "I think I'm going to lose my job over this. I walked out in front of all the other reps. My boss probably didn't like it."

The next morning, my boss met me outside the meeting room, and he asked if we could go for a walk. I figured this was it. I was going to pack my bags, head home, and look for another job. When we got outside, he turned to me and said, "Michael, I want you to know that in no way do I hold what happened last night against you. In fact, I respect it. When I was younger, I was in youth ministry, so I really respect your stand." I breathed a sigh of relief.

When I'd been a pastor for a couple of years, I had a dream one night. It was about a pretty girl in the church's youth group. It wasn't a sexual dream, but when I woke up, I felt very awkward about it. I didn't even know the girl, but I guess I'd seen her a time or two. I thought it must have been the pizza I'd had for supper. But I had the same dream the next night. I believed that I'd be safe only if I didn't tell them—darkness is the enemy's territory.

> I believed that I'd be safe only if I didn't tell them—darkness is the enemy's territory.

By this time, I knew that I needed a friend or two who could know the worst about me and still be my friend. One of them was Brian, my pastor, and the other was Nabi Saleh, the founder of Gloria Jeans. Before I called them, the thought leaped into my brain like a hungry tiger: If I tell them, I'll be kicked out of the ministry! The enemy was working overtime. I hadn't done anything, and I didn't even know the girl, but I'd had two dreams about her. I decided to tell Valery. It was really hard for her to hear it. She cried because it brought up all of her issues around the fear of rejection about her dad, who died when she was nineteen, and her first husband, who walked out on her, but it was ultimately good for each of us and our relationship. I told Brian the next morning, and I talked to Nabi a few days later. Two weeks later, I was in the office doing some copying when the girl walked in. Obviously, she had no idea about my dreams, but I left right away. It took about a month to get the thoughts out of my system. Being honest with Valery, Brian, and Nabi was the best solution. Talking to them short-circuited the flow of temptation, and I'm not sure I'd be in ministry today if I hadn't been honest with them.

I hope you don't have strongholds, but if you do, they may be very different from mine. There are two major categories: sins and wounds. The way we've hurt people and our unwillingness to repent and ask for forgiveness create a powerfully poisonous force in our hearts. And the unresolved, unhealed, ungrieved wounds inflicted on us are like living with a gangrenous open wound. And, of course, the categories aren't quite so neat and tidy: hurt people hurt people, so they almost always overlap.

To find real freedom, we need a pair of strategies: remove and invest. To remove the racing, negative thoughts, we first must identify them and then replace them with the truth. To remove the effects of past wounds, we have to face the hurt head-on and enter the process of grieving and forgiving. To remove the guilt of past sins, we need to avoid excusing ourselves, minimizing the damage we've caused, or denying that it even happened, admit what we've done, ask for forgiveness, and seek reconciliation.

We invest in the bank account of our souls when we deposit the truths of our identity in Christ, find acceptance and affirmation from Him and from a few trusted people, listen to music that feeds our hearts, and spend time relaxing with people so we can begin to learn to be ourselves.

How do we do this? Let me be very prescriptive: Speak assertively to your soul! Many of the Psalms aren't praise, they aren't prayers, and they aren't laments—they're holy self-talk. Look at a few when David let us hear him talking to himself:

> *Why are you cast down, O my soul?*
> *And why are you disquieted within me?*
> *Hope in God, for I shall yet praise Him*
> *For the help of His countenance.*
> —Psalms 42:5
> *My soul, wait silently for God alone,*
> *For my expectation is from Him.*
> *He only is my rock and my salvation;*

He is my defense;
I shall not be moved.
In God is my salvation and my glory;
The rock of my strength,
And my refuge, is in God.
—Psalms 62:5-7

Bless the LORD, *O my soul;*
And all that is within me, bless His holy name!
Bless the LORD, *O my soul,*
And forget not all His benefits:
Who forgives all your iniquities,
Who heals all your diseases,
Who redeems your life from destruction,
Who crowns you with lovingkindness and tender mercies,
Who satisfies your mouth with good things,
So that your youth is renewed like the eagle's.
—Psalms 103:1-5

Memorize these (and others), and give yourself a good talking to when you're discouraged, tempted, afraid, or filled with guilt and shame. They are keys to unlock the strongholds in our hearts.

Many of us can trace our deepest sins and hurts to how we were treated when we were children, to trauma when we were older (like the sexual abuse I suffered), or the heartbreak of losing a spouse or a child, to name just a few examples. We can see a direct relational and emotional connection to those people and events, but we need to remember the spiritual component: the enemy of our souls hates us, he's a liar, and he uses deception, temptation, and accusation to beat us down. I believe God wants us to be delivered from the enemy's schemes and his grip. Years ago, deliverance ministries were often considered out of the mainstream and, to be honest, weird. But today, we're seeing the Holy Spirit promise and provide deliverance in very healthy ways. Freedom is for all believers. Certainly, not all of us are in the same kind of bondage, but all of us are buffeted by lies, distortions, and condemnation that find their source in the father of lies.

Strongholds are different from passing phases. For instance, a person may get angry for being cut off in traffic, but it passes. In contrast, a spirit of anger is deeper, stronger, and more consuming. Similarly, fear, doubt, self-hatred, and bitterness are common strongholds. They're often coupled with deep wounds that haven't healed, so the solution is both healing and repentance.

When a person practices these self- and other-destructive behaviors for a long time, it's like digging a channel for water to flow. It doesn't change direction very easily! We need to be diligent and patient to dig a new mental channel, feasting on the truth of God's Word and assertively, confidently speaking truth to our souls. Near the beginning of the book, in "Formula 1," I described the importance of "owning your morning." I'm a fanatic about it because it gets me going in the right direction from the moment I wake up. I'm responsible to put myself in the hands of God every morning. Most days, it's a delightful spiritual and emotional experience, but every day, I need to be reminded of who I am and whose I am . . . because it's so easy to drift into dangerous waters. We're in a battle every day. Paul put it this way: "I say then: Walk in the Spirit, and you shall not fulfill the lust of the flesh. For the flesh lusts against the Spirit, and the Spirit against the flesh; and these are contrary to one another, so that you do not do the things that you wish" (Galatians 5:16-17). He then contrasts "the works of the flesh" and "the fruit of the Spirit"—one is the product of selfishness and the counterfeit gods; the other is organically produced from the inside out. He ends with a fact, an invitation, and a warning: "And those *who* are Christ's have crucified the flesh with its passions and desires. If we live in the Spirit, let us also walk in the Spirit. Let us not become conceited, provoking one another, envying one another" (vs. 24-26). Why does he need to warn us again? Because we're so fragile and susceptible to the enemy's lies. We need to make it a habit of removing the passions of the flesh—whether sex or bitterness or jealousy or . . . —and replacing them with the love, joy, power, and freedom found only in God's grace and His Word.

The law said, "Don't think like that!" But grace says, "My child, think about My love for you." In other words, we can't overcome destructive thoughts through self-condemnation. If someone tells me, "Michael, stop thinking about a pink elephant in purple pants carrying a green parasol!" what am I going to think about? Right. But then, if I hear someone say, "Now think about a blue giraffe wearing a red coat on a skateboard," I've replaced one with the other. It's the same for our thinking: I can either listen to the condemning, shaming, doubting voices rooted in past sins and wounds and reinforced by the enemy, or I can hear God say, "Come to Me, you who are weary and heavy laden, and I'll give you rest." Replacing one with the other changes the direction of my thinking. We experience tremendous power and relief by confessing the nature of God and the promises of His Word.

Just this morning, as I prepared my heart for the day, I thought of the old song, "Turn your eyes upon Jesus. Look full in His wonderful face, and the things of earth will grow strangely dim in the light of His glory and grace." The things of earth are the idols, the traps we can so easily fall into. It takes time to prepare our hearts. I know, I've heard it a thousand times: you're busy, you're doing all this for God, and you can't spare the time because people are going to hell and you've got to get to work. Here's what I think about that: Bosh! We are first and foremost children of the King, the apple of His eye, the delight of His heart. If we don't take time to soak in His great love and His infinite wisdom, we may be really busy, but we may forget why we're doing so much so fast.

Remove and replace negative thoughts, and invest your heart in God's proclamation of His great love for you. This will set you up every day to walk in the Spirit and as His extremely loved child under the authority of the Lordship of Christ.

Those who are wounded and broken reproduce themselves as they lead and keep their focus on their hurts instead of releasing them to focus on God and the disciple-making mission He wants to entrust to all of us. *XLR8*'s promise is that God will set you free to be all you can be for Him and His kingdom. Don't let past wounds and sins cloud your thinking, erode your joy, and distract you from experiencing the love, forgiveness, and power of God.

The owners, engineers, mechanics, and drivers in Formula 1 racing are meticulous in making sure nothing is slowing down their car. Are ungrieved hurts or unrepented sins weighing you down? Is your soul in bondage? It's time to be set free.

PIT STOP

Paul wrote to the Corinthians, "For though we walk in the flesh, we do not war according to the flesh. For the weapons of our warfare are not carnal but mighty in God for pulling down strongholds, casting down arguments and every high thing that exalts itself against the knowledge of God, bringing every thought into captivity to the obedience of Christ" (2 Corinthians 10:3-5).

1) What does it mean to "war according to the flesh"?
2) How can you "cast down arguments and every high thing that exalts itself against the knowledge of God"? In other words, what are the thoughts you need to remove?

3) As you've read this chapter, has the Spirit pointed out any strongholds?
4) How will you invest more productively in your soul?
5) Go back to "Formula 1" and look again at "Own Your Morning." What difference has it made if you've been practicing this? What difference will it make if you start?

"Now the Lord had said to Abram: 'Get out of your country, from your family and from your father's house, to a land that I will show you. I will make you a great nation; I will bless you and make your name great; and you shall be a blessing. I will bless those who bless you, and I will curse him who curses you; and in you all the families of the earth shall be blessed.'"

—Genesis 12:1–3

EIGHTH GEAR: FUND YOUR VISION

Many years ago, when our kids were little, one of our favorite vacation destinations was Fraser Island off Queensland's beautiful Sunshine Coast. Apart from being the largest sand island in the world, with over sixty miles (100 kms) of beach driving, it's home to some breathtaking, pristine, turquoise-colored freshwater lakes. Our first trip there was somewhat of an adventure, to say the least. I'd recently picked up a brand new royal blue Toyota Four Runner.

I couldn't wait to get in some exciting sand driving—but I was clueless about any sort of 4WDing, especially during high tide—no one told me you had to let air out of your tires when we landed on the beach leading up where the ferry headed out from the mainland. Such was the trauma of the soft sand beach driving that I had to get behind a guy who was driving a beaten-up old Army Jeep. It sure looked like he knew what he was doing. We were slogging it out on this sand and got bogged down a few times. It was tough going.

A little further on, we came to a short isthmus of sand where the water was just starting to lap over. This was a "shortcut" saving us the forty-five-minute drive to go back around via the road. Valery could smell trouble and pleaded with me not to drive across the one hundred yards of wet sand. As a dutiful husband, I got out and walked through it, looking back somewhat smugly to my "freaked out" family. All was going well till I hit a patch of quicksand! In an instant, I was up to my waist. Had I driven through, I would have put the family at grave risk and been over my head in water. (Cue red face.)

On another occasion, one of my best buddies missed a sudden bend in the road whilst careening down a long hill near his house. Rather than stick to the road, he plowed his car through a flimsy fence and right into a creek. He quickly climbed out as the vehicle sank up to its roof. He was lucky he wasn't badly injured. Ultimately, there was no harm done except a waterlogged car and his dented pride.

So many pastors are in over their heads financially or at least are paddling hard to keep their heads above water. I've never had a conversation with a pastor who told me, "Michael, we have more money than we need." If that ever happens, I'm going to say, "Dude, you need a bigger vision!" Every pastor I've met with—and I mean everyone—has said they could do more for the Kingdom of God if they had more resources, and specifically money. They need more money to reach the lost, they need more money to help the poor, they need more money to train leaders, they need more money to provide the very best children's ministry, and they need money for every other vision God puts on their hearts.

THEOLOGY, SOCIOLOGY, AND PSYCHOLOGY

We need to understand the distinction between the Giver and the givers. We need a solid theology about God's generosity and delight in providing for His children. We also need a solid sociology and psychology to understand what motivates our people to give generously because they really want to. In the early days of my ministry experience, the prevailing thought was: "Yes, we need money, but we don't want too much because it can cause all kinds of problems." The paucity of our theology limited our vision for impact. One person on our team came from a Salvation Army background, so "fundraising" was carrying a red bucket to the streets and pubs to ask for a few coins. They do wonderful work, but their strategy for raising money usually left them needing much more—except for the occasional very generous bill put in the bucket. I understand. Our family was poor. My parents, six siblings, and I lived in my grandmother's house. It had only three bedrooms, so my Dad closed in the porch and made it my bedroom. I had a lot to learn about God's perspective of money.

> We need to understand the distinction between the Giver and the givers.

Not long after Valery and I got married and I joined the church staff, I suddenly realized what I'd done: As a pharmaceutical product manager, I made a good salary and had a company car, but now, my salary was sliced down to a nub. Even when I made money, I certainly didn't manage it well. When we got married, Valery brought assets she'd saved from her career as a flight attendant, and I brought considerable liabilities—I concluded it was a match made in heaven! (I'm not sure she had the same thought.) The church was growing fast, and we needed a bigger building, so we launched a building campaign. I had no experience with anything like that, and Valery grew up with her lovely Cornish mum in the Church of England. The last building campaign they started was in the late sixteenth century! Valery and her mum had some serious misgivings about me. Valery had married a businessman who was headed to the top. On the day I resigned, my bosses had been discussing sending me to Switzerland to enter a leadership accelerator that would have seen me rapidly promoted and would have brought a big raise. They asked what I was going to do, and I explained that I was going to join a church staff to help the church grow. They offered to "sweeten" the deal for me, but I told them, "This isn't about negotiating a better deal. I'm called to be part of what this church is doing." Valery and I had been poised to be on the gravy train, but we'd done a U-turn financially and were scraping just to get by. When we sat down and wrote out our budget, we were eight dollars in the hole every week. Somehow, God provided and we didn't go into debt. Actually, I received a check from Pfizer for some vacation time I hadn't taken. I told Valery, "We're going to have some fun with this on a really lovely holiday... because it may be the last one we ever have." She was happy about it.

Several years later, after being portable for a decade, the growth in the church dictated it was time to build our own facility. The brochures for our building campaign came back from the printer. I had helped design them, so I brought one home to show Valery. I put it on the bedside table in our room, and when I came back a little later, it was on the floor. She really struggled with the idea of us giving a significant portion of our meager income to a building campaign, but God began to work in her heart (and mine). We've participated in many more building campaigns over the years, and she has been known to double what I plan to give.

It took some time for me to grasp the theology of God's gracious generosity. Among the important passages that changed my perspective, God used the initial call of Abraham (then, Abram):

> *Now the Lord had said to Abram:*
> *"Get out of your country,*
> *From your family*
> *And from your father's house,*
> *To a land that I will show you.*
> *I will make you a great nation;*
> *I will bless you*
> *And make your name great;*
> *And you shall be a blessing.*
> *I will bless those who bless you,*
> *And I will curse him who curses you;*
> *And in you all the families of the earth shall be blessed."*
> —Genesis 12:1-3

God blesses us, but not for our own comfort and prestige. He makes us a channel of His generosity so He can use us to bless others. That's how the lost are reached; that's how the poor are cared for; that's how believers make an impact on their communities. God doesn't have a problem with His children having money, but He has a big problem with our money having a grip on us.

Years later, when I was the pastor at ShireLive, we needed more space. For a while, I talked boldly about the vision of building a larger facility so we could reach and disciple more people. As long as the vision was down the road, I felt great about it. As things got more crowded, it was time to initiate a building campaign. Now, the vague ideas about growing were becoming very specific and concrete (literally concrete). By this time, I knew the drill, so we carefully plotted out our strategy and timeline. Everyone was on board, and the plans were rolling out. But one night, I woke up in a cold sweat. I realized I didn't have the faith to believe God for this money. I thought, *I'm the pastor! What am I going to do?*

I desperately sought out a pastor who had a gift in the area of finances. Ian Zerna was a genius with construction and financing. I asked him to meet me. When we sat down, I told him bluntly, "Ian, I'm in trouble."

He'd solved enough problems in his day to not be rattled by my declaration. He asked, "Michael, what's wrong?"

When I told him about my lack of faith, he didn't chastise me; instead, he told me stories of seemingly hopeless situations that turned out better than anyone expected. As he talked, I felt new waves of faith infused into my soul. I didn't have any more money, but God had used Ian to restore my faith that He would provide.

Not long after my meeting with Ian, I was once again awake in the middle of the night, this time praying, not fretting. As I was asking God for guidance, He gave me a burst of creativity, and I started writing my thoughts down. We needed to raise about $5 million over three years for the $13 million project. We'd borrow the rest. I thought, *What if one person gave half a million, a couple of others gave $200 thousand, several gave $100 thousand, and a bunch of people gave $50 thousand?* I felt emboldened by the Holy Spirit and the faith God had put in my heart to make a big ask.

We held a meeting for our "Kingdom Builders," those individuals, couples, and families who had committed to give more than a tithe to special projects. I told them, "I'll never ask anyone to give a specific amount, but let me explain how God might move in our lives to provide the money we need for our new building. For example, there may be someone here tonight who wants to give half a million dollars. [My voice cracked when I said it.] Others might give $200 thousand, or $100 thousand, or $50 thousand." Prior to this, the largest gift given to our church had been $20,000! I had no idea how these people would respond.

After the meeting, one of our elders walked up and announced, "I think I'm your half-a-million guy."

For some very strange reason, I didn't just hug him and celebrate his generosity. Instead, out of my mouth came a question, "Why do you want to give that much?" Instantly I thought, *What the heck am I doing? I should have thanked him, taken the money, and run!* I followed up by asking him, "Is it just for me, or is it for the Lord?"

But God used my question in a way I hadn't imagined. We talked for a minute or two, and then I told him, "Go home, talk to your wife, and pray about it together. If you still feel it's God's leading, go for it."

He called me a few days later and said, "Pastor Michael, we're in."

As he gave, God blessed him even more—far more abundantly than he could have asked or thought! God doesn't always bless financially. He's more creative than that. But He sure blessed this man's obedience to be generous . . . and He blessed my obedience to speak it to our Kingdom Builders. During our building campaigns, we pledged to never pull back from our involvement in global missions. It was part of our DNA from the beginning.

When I consult with pastors, especially if our conversation turns to buildings and finances, I ask them, "What do you believe about money?" Their answers tell me volumes about their theological, philosophical, and psychological grasp of the Giver and the givers. Jesus had a lot to say about money, and He used finances in many of His parables to illustrate points (such as the story in Matthew 18 about the servant who owed ten thousand talents . . . a parable to show that those who don't feel forgiven don't forgive others). A person's perspective on money is an integral part of discipleship because it both exposes what's in the heart and reinforces the heart's inclinations—for good or ill. Humans have several blatant vulnerabilities: sex, power, and money are three that are most commonly mentioned.

Generosity is insurance against the soul being corrupted by the thirst for wealth. Individual believers and those collectively gathered as churches are never meant to be lakes dammed up but flowing rivers of resources flowing to those in need. God's grace is free, but sowing seed and bringing in the harvest costs money.

I believe God is looking for faithful leaders to entrust an abundance of resources, but the proviso is generosity in the heart of the pastor and a culture of generosity among the people. If these things aren't present, an abundance of resources will feed our comparison and competition, and our hearts will be corrupted.

Our theology is rooted in the nature of God, who was infinitely generous in giving His Son to die in our place and loves to bless His children. Our sociology helps us understand that generosity is contagious—just like stinginess and the idolatry of wealth. And our psychology is based on the fact that people want their lives to count, so we can appeal to their best selves to invite them to join us on the adventure of expanding the kingdom. Just as God has put the gift of evangelism in the lives of perhaps ten percent of a congregation, He has probably put the gift of giving in the hearts of a similar number. The question for pastors who lead people with these gifts is simple but often absent: "How are you stewarding these people and their gifts?"

GOALS AND BENCHMARKS

As I've worked with pastors to help them create a culture of generosity, almost all of them have seen dramatic results. Within a year, tithes and offerings increased an average of just over thirty percent, and giving above the tithe grew by over seventy percent. (To be fair, some of them had never encouraged people to give more than the tithe, so they began from a standing start.) In two or three years, I've seen churches double their giving—without a shred of manipulation or coercion.

But let's not get lost in the numbers. The goal isn't the money; the goal is making disciples who use everything God has put in their hands, tangible and intangible, to expand the kingdom to the glory of God.

> **The goal isn't the money; the goal is making disciples who use everything God has put in their hands, tangible and intangible, to expand the kingdom to the glory of God.**

A lot of pastors speak the narrative, "Our people are incredibly generous!" . . . and these pastors believe it, even when it isn't quite true. One of my jobs is to burst their bubble by providing empirical data. In the vast majority of cases, the data shows that their people aren't nearly as generous as they thought. For instance, when a pastor made that remark to me, I asked, "That's wonderful. Do you think there's much left on the table?"

He inevitably says, "Oh, yeah, I'm sure there's some."

I probe, "Would you mind if we do a little quick analysis?" (How can he say "no"?) So I continue: "Let's say there are a thousand people in the life of the church." (He nods.) "So, we can assume there are about 300 giving units. Is that about right?" (Another nod.) Actually, if there are a thousand on a given Sunday, there are almost certainly 2000 people who are considered "regular attenders," making about 600 giving units, but I don't push it yet. I ask, "What's the average income in your area?"

Most pastors know that number, so he says, "About $70 thousand, and many are dual-income homes."

"Let's just stick with the $70 thousand. So, if the 300 giving units tithe $7 thousand, that's $2.1 million." I let that sink in and then ask, "What was your church's income last year?"

"Just over $1.3 million."

"What could you do to help a bunch more people and to expand the kingdom of God with $800 thousand more?"

His eyes widen, and he exclaims, "A lot!"

"Now, you won't get all of that because not everyone will tithe if you ask them to, but many will, and some will give more than the tithe. Remember, I'm not making these numbers up. You gave them to me. I'm just doing a little calculation." I let him think about that a bit, and then I asked, "Do you think God is withholding His blessings that much? No, I don't think so. But there are some things you can do to communicate God's command to tithe and tap into the generosity of your people for over and above giving. Let's talk about that."

I go to great lengths to explain that I'm not suggesting they strongarm anyone or use guilt to manipulate them to give. When Jesus said, "Follow me," He summons us to follow in every aspect of our lives, to honor Him in the boardroom and the bedroom, with the boss and with the kids, with the people He has put around us and the resources He has put in our hands. Our use of money is just another aspect of submitting to the Lordship of Christ.

I wouldn't say that I am the building campaign expert, but I've been part of enough of them—those I led and those led by pastors who have asked me to consult with them—that I've seen some patterns. In general, in their first building campaign, pastors can expect people to give up to seventy percent over their usual giving over three years. So a church with an annual budget of a million can expect to receive $700 thousand in additional giving over those years. Or aside from a building campaign, churches have all kinds of other projects that need to be funded—missions, camps, counseling centers, food distribution, etc. If the over-and-above giving for the church with a budget of $1 million is thirty percent (instead of seventy), they'll have $300 thousand to invest in these life-changing programs.

Asks for building campaigns are often more productive than asks for missions because the givers can expect to benefit directly from the results. I'm not being cynical, just observant. They'll enjoy the new auditorium with better lighting and sound, their little children will have a great time in the new kids' area, and their teenagers will be attracted to the new youth room. In other words, there's a personal payoff. A step of maturity beyond the personal payoff is giving to something like Kingdom Builders and trusting the pastor to distribute the money as the God-appointed steward. When people give to build an orphanage in Kenya, a well in Ethiopia, or a church in Indonesia, they may never get to see it, so faith is required to give to meet those needs. Similarly, generational giving requires the same level of maturity and faith. When people give to a Christian college to endow a chair, they may never meet the students, and they may never know the stories of the impact the students have after they graduate and enter the secular world as light and salt or go into the ministry as those who announce the Good News, but their impact is very real. When they give to fund research for a medical breakthrough, they will probably never meet the doctors and scientists, and they won't hear the names of the people whose lives are saved, but they can be sure they've made a difference.

CAPITAL POTENTIAL

I talk to pastors about their "capital potential." We're still using the church with an annual budget of $1 million as our example. A good rule of thumb is to dedicate one-third to the salaries of the pastor and staff, one-third to facilities, and the remaining third to operations, projects, etc. In the first year, with an emphasis on obedience to tithe and generosity above and beyond to build a new facility, they raise an additional half a million. Where does the $1.5 million go? We'll assume the church will have the same staff members, so they allocate the same $330 thousand to salaries, operations remain at $330 thousand, and facilities will be funded with the original third and the additional money, a total of $830 thousand. These numbers don't count on any growth, but let's say the church grows by ten percent a year for ten years. After the first year, even with growth, giving isn't quite as strong as the first year, maybe an additional $400 thousand over and above for the next four years, so the facilities are allocated $830, $730, $730, $730, and $730, or roughly $3.75 million. This is the number you show your bank when you apply for a loan. When you show your giving history, and they crunch the numbers, you'll probably be able to borrow north of $12 million.

As lead pastors, our responsibility extends beyond the vision God has entrusted to us. It's also our God-given task to disciple the givers and steward the gifts donated to fulfill the vision. God has given us the high privilege to disciple the people He loves. Paul wrote his protégé Timothy about how to use the Word in discipleship, and we can apply it directly to money: "All Scripture is given by inspiration of God, and is profitable for doctrine, for reproof, for correction, for instruction in righteousness, that the man of God may be complete, thoroughly equipped for every good work" (2 Timothy 3:16-17). Are we using the Word of God to teach, reprove, correct, and train our people in their relationships, their character, their devotion, their work, prayer, Bible study, evangelism, and every other aspect of their lives? Of course we are. We need to disciple them just as much in their perspectives and use of money as these other vital elements of their lives.

XLR8's promise is that as you obey the Great commission and genuinely Disciple your people, that God will lead you to create an environment where people give more—often much more—because their hearts are captured with the vision of making a difference for God and His kingdom. Don't settle for less.

The boss of the pit crew on a Formula 1 team is responsible to train, motivate, and equip the crew to function at peak performance. Together, they make it happen. Similarly, I believe God has entrusted His people with the means to fulfill His loving will in every local community and throughout the world . . . if we will teach them that they are blessed to be a blessing. Our people are gold in the mountain and diamonds in the mine. Our responsibility is to dig deep and draw generosity out of their hearts and release them to be all God has called them to be.

PIT STOP

FINANCIAL STRENGTH DIAGNOSTIC

*(1 is a definitive, not where we want to be and
5 is totally where we want to be.)*

1) PRAYER

We have built a strong foundation of prayer that covers the vision and provision of our church.

    1   2   3   4   5

2) GRATITUDE

We say thank you and show Gratitude toward first-time and Givers.

    1   2   3   4   5

3) ENCOUNTER

We Relentlessly Pursue powerful Encounters and Transformation for all people.

    1   2   3   4   5

4) UNITY

We have a strong sense and reality of relational and missional unity from the Elders, Pastors, and Leaders through to the congregation members.

    1   2   3   4   5

5) TRUTH

We Courageously Impart the Truth of God's Word about finance and stewardship.

    1   2   3   4   5

6) SERIES

We preach a series on giving and generosity each year, which we also carry through and integrate through our Small Groups.

    1   2   3   4   5

7) ENGAGEMENT

We are Building a strong Community of Market Place Leaders.

    1   2   3   4   5

8) GENERATIONS

We have a vibrant ministry to children and teens to which they regularly bring their friends.

    1   2   3   4   5

9) MINISTRY

We are leading a ministry that sees people transformed by the power and Word of God.

    1   2   3   4   5

10) GROUPS

We have a well-developed and effective Small Group ministry that has built genuine connectedness amongst the hearts and lives of the people.

1   2   3   4   5

11) DISCIPLESHIP

We make and hold a clear Connection between Stewardship and Discipleship.

1   2   3   4   5

12) CELEBRATION

We conduct weekend services at our church that are Christ-centred, Bible-based, and accommodating of both guests and those already committed to the church.

1   2   3   4   5

13) COMMUNITY

We meet real and desperate needs in both our local community and in the nations.

1   2   3   4   5

14) INTENTIONALITY

We minister to and partner intentionally with Business and Marketplace Leaders in our church.

1   2   3   4   5

15) VISION

We carry a vision that captivates and resonates with the people in our church.

1   2   3   4   5

16) STRATEGY

We align our financial budget with our church strategy with resources allocated for maximum kingdom impact and fruitfulness.

    1   2   3   4   5

17) TRANSPARENCY

We operate with financial transparency and accountability which builds great trust amongst the people.

    1   2   3   4   5

18) FRUITFULNESS

We have a demonstrated track record of strong Ministry Fruitfulness.

    1   2   3   4   5

19) THE LEAST

We Minister effectively to the "least," the poor, and the vulnerable in our community.

    1   2   3   4   5

20) KINGDOM BUILDERS

We have developed a strong Kingdom Builders ministry who understand that part of their reason for existing is to resource the Kingdom of God.

    1   2   3   4   5

HOW TO INCREASE YOUR CHURCH'S FINANCIAL STRENGTH BY 40% IN TWO YEARS!

Your Comprehensive Roadmap

1) Take An Objective Assessment Of Your Current Financial Situation And Trajectory.
    - » Track the money spent to ensure that waste is minimized and good stewardship is maximized.

2) Stake Your Claim To God's Promise Of Provision For His Kingdom Mission.
   » Stand against the spirit of intimidation.
   » Bring the truth of God's Word on money.

3) Forsake The Habit Of Eating All Your Seed And Build A Faith Margin To Sow Into Your Future Vision.
   » This is a faith issue, not just a financial one.
   » Your faith for the future is evidenced by your willingness to allocate resources toward it.

4) Shake-Up Your Budget To Realign Your Spending With Your Strategic Priorities.
   » Do a careful analysis of resource allocation and return on investment.

5) Make A Review Of Your Visionary Fire Power And Assess Your Ministry's Transformational Impact.
    » People respond positively and generously when the ministry has a tangible transformational impact on people.

    _____
    _____
    _____

6) Wake Up The Company Of Believers Who Possess A Gift Of Giving And Develop A Kingdom Builders Ministry.
    » Exhort these kb's to be all in for the kingdom, to spend quality time with Jesus daily, have the back of their pastors and leaders, and pray with their spouse every day.

    _____
    _____
    _____

7) Break Through The False Ceiling Blocking God's Abundant Supply Chain With A Spirit Of Faith That Matches The Immensity Of The Harvest Challenge.
    » Daily develop your faith in the Word and confession.

    _____
    _____
    _____

Where Does The 40% Come From?
- 15% TandO
- 15% KB's
- 10% Saving
- 10% Margin

Some Financial Benchmarks
- Work out Church Giving Potential
  - Number of family units
  - Average family income/yr
  - Take a tithe of that
  - Do the math against your current giving.
  - Get mad at the devil and be encouraged as to the potential.
- Average giving per head is between $25 and $50 a week.
- Extra Giving can be between 30 and 70% of your TandO.
- Check your 1/3;1/3;1/3 Ratios.
- Your Building Financing Capacity
  - TandO $500k
  - Facilities Ratio 1/3 = $150k
  - Future Fund 1/10 = $50k
  - Extra KB Giving = $150k
  - Total for facilities = $350k

WORKSHEET ON GENEROSITY

1) What is your church's average weekly attendance?
2) How many giving units do you have?
3) What is the average household income (sometimes one earner, sometimes two) for your community?
   Giving units X average household income = _____
   A tithe of this amount: _____
   Divide that total by 52 weeks: _____ This is your potential tithe from your people.
   Your last year's annual income: _____
   Divide that by 52 weeks: _____ This is the actual giving of your people.

Subtract the actual giving/week _____ from potential tithe/week _____ = _____

What does this exercise tell you?

What's your plan to increase the level of cheerful giving at your church?

PEDAL TO THE METAL

A lot of pastors die on the hill of good intentions. Good ideas, even godly ideas, without execution go nowhere, and in fact, they erode the credibility of the one who promises more than he delivers. What is execution? Contacts, appointments, meetings, and culture—this is where we get traction with our people as we move them toward the goal.

All of the concepts in this book are rooted in biblical truths and the proven experience of pastors who have applied them. We don't have to try it alone. We're part of a body, and pastors need encouragement, understanding, and support as much (or more) as anyone. We're on the cutting edge, leaving it all on the field every day. It's very easy to become exhausted and discouraged. We need someone—a close friend, a coach, a counselor, or a mentor—to come alongside us to remind us what's most important, that we have the resources of heaven at our disposal, and we have a God who is crazy about us.

For Formula 1 drivers, there's nothing like the feeling of flying around the track at top speed. In the same way, we are never more fulfilled than when we feel the wind of God in our wings. As we daily, weekly, and monthly pursue the call God has put on our hearts, and we sense His Spirit at work in, around, and through us, we live with that beautiful blend of passion and peace—we wake up each day asking, "God, what do You have for me today?" But we're compelled by love, not driven by comparison and competition. We can run wide open, the pedal to the metal, in our thrilling ride with God, trusting Him to do what only He can do, resting in His presence, experiencing His power, and watching Him transform individuals, families, and communities.

On this side of heaven, there's nothing better.

ABOUT THE AUTHOR

Pastors are heroes to us, it's that simple! With a passion to support leaders in both the church and the marketplace to be everything God intended them to be, LEADERSCAPE was launched in 2013.

Begun by Michael and Valery, LEADERSCAPE quenched this burden to support God's Generals, as they partner with the Holy Spirit, to catalyze accelerated momentum in their churches.

There was a need to get beyond courses or personal encouragement (though we are all over both of these), to deliver tangible and measurable results. With actual outcomes for real churches of 30%, 50% or 100% growth in less than eighteen months, what LEADERSCAPE offers has now been thoroughly validated.

From the small beginnings on their kitchen table, where Valery ran all the operations and support and Michael did the outreach, content creation, and coaching... things have come a long way. The LEADERSCAPE team currently reaches out to over 1,000 Pastors each week and dispatches templates and training resources to that same number every month.

They now support Pastors through both their in-person and online coaching programs, their XLR8 Podcast, and now with the XLR8 book getting into the hands of ten thousand Lead Pastors, their strategic influence is progressing.

By continuing to deliver these game-changing solutions to thousands of Pastors, Michael and Valery have a vision to help one million believers get intentionally discipled over the next several years.

The consulting side of LEADERSCAPE sees the convergence of Michael's experience in the non-profit sector, initially as the Associate Minister of Hills CLC church (which later became Hillsong), for their first twelve years, then as Senior Pastor of Shirelive, in Sydney's south, for twelve years. At Shirelive, Valery was a force in discipling women. She started with just a few ladies groups only to see these explode to 125 dynamic groups within thirty months.

Michael also served in both State and National denominational leadership roles for two decades with the Australian Christian Churches, helping to lead the Church planting and health initiatives for over 1,000 churches.

He has also been the Chancellor and Chair of the Council of Alphacrucis University College for the past ten years.

Partners of LEADERSCAPE benefit from forty years of leadership experience and extensive cross-cultural ministry along with an unshakable desire to see pastors actually achieve the dream that God has put in their hearts.

Now expanding rapidly, LEADERSCAPE is journeying toward its global vision of providing programs in ten languages. With its resources currently available in English and Spanish, we have many more to come. LEADERSCAPE is also raising up a team of coaches which help scale the ministry ultimately equipping thousands of pastors to double their churches and become the disciple-making Pastors they always dreamed of being.

Michael and Valery travel extensively outside of Australia to coach the 'Face to Face' LEADERSCAPE partners, whom they are privileged to serve.

Every church and every pastor is important and highly valued.

LEADERSCAPE is every pastor's friend.... And they love them!

FOR LEAD PASTORS ONLY

I lost my virginity in the back of a VW. This impulsive decision stemmed from my sexual abuse by a man at age fourteen and my decision to "go it alone" to prove my heterosexuality rather than reach out for help. As I indicated earlier, this promiscuous season cost me and many others quite a lot of heartache. Stacks of people were hurt as I tried to sort out my stuff all by myself.

A similar outcome happened when I transitioned into ShireLive Church as Lead Pastor. Rather than reach out for help from someone further down the track who had fresh eyes and a bit more grey hair, I went it alone . . . again. My internal narrative was everything from:

- "I got this!" to . . .
- "I know what to do!" and
- "I sense God is about to do something big!"
- "I've done it once (Hillsong), and I can do it again here" (This was the dominant self-talk of vain assurance.)

As I reflect back on many of the mistakes I made, I don't think I was listening. I was praying a heap, but I think I was filtering even God's voice according to my preconceptions. I assured myself that everything was fine—in fact, great! But I had so many blind spots that

I looked like a leopard! I hurt a lot of people, people I loved. Heaps of people left our church, and if I'm honest, I blamed that on them!

One day, whilst driving past a group of mums from our church (frankly, not members of my fan club at the time) who were having a chat, I imagined they were talking about me, my leadership, and all the problems in our church!

I craned my neck to look back at the bus stop at these ladies to try to eavesdrop on their "gossip," but when I heard their conversation, I quickly realized I wasn't the center of their attention at all. They were just talking about the beautiful day, their kids, and what they did over the weekend. My insecurity was doing crazy things in my head! I had been so preoccupied with their thoughts about me, I didn't notice the car in front of me had stopped! Yup! You're getting ahead of me...

I plowed into the back of the now stationary vehicle!

As I pulled over to the side of the road to chat with my victim, feeling embarrassed and ashamed, the Holy Spirit spoke to me: "As long as you continue to look back, Michael, you'll continue to run into things!" Ouch! But I knew He was right!

I'm an optimist, which has served me well in many seasons, but my positive outlook blinded me to what wasn't happening—I was ignoring the trajectory of my life, trying to tell great stories so people would be impressed with me, and focused on the wrong metrics.

I was addicted to anecdotes because I was allergic to empirics!

By definition, I didn't recognize my blind spots. I needed a different set of eyes, someone who could see the truth about me and cared enough to speak that truth in love. I made one of the best decisions of my life: I reached out for help.

In *XLR8*, we're offering a bunch of laser-focused resources to help you to catalyze fresh momentum in your church. But that's not all. We are also making a limited offer for a select few lead pastors to apply for the offer of all offers: a totally free Strategic Ministry Zoom Call with my Head Coach, including a comprehensive Church Health, Discipleship, and Momentum Assessment.

Simply go to the QR Code and answer a few simple questions. I hope you'll be one of the lead pastors who take advantage of this offer.

ONE MILLION DISCIPLES 2030

THE DIVINE DESIGN

This past season, has seen a Divine set up for an extra-ordinary move of God's Spirit through the church.

- We are carrying the deep burden of many tired Pastors around the globe, some who would like to quit & others who feel stuck on the wrong side of their dream fulfillment.
- We believe God has given us a prophetic mandate & the tools to radically help.

After 10 years & 10,000 hrs working with Lead Pastors & their teams, we now have our Disciple Making program XLR8 tightly dialed in and effective.

- In the past 2 years alone, we've seen some strong results as churches lock & load our XLR8 program, with 30, 50 & 100% growth in under 18mths.
- With the launch of this *XLR8* book, is now time to scale what we are doing, to support 10,000 pastors in their Disciple- Making endeavors.

ONE MILLION DISCIPLES

A combination of this *XLR8* book, our catalytic XLR8 program, and our new XLR8 Podcast, will advance our mandate to significantly lift 10,000 Pastors to be the Disciple-Making Pastors they always dreamed of being.

As each pastor engages just 100 believers in intentional discipleship (though many will blow this out of the water)—that's One Million Disciples... One Million!

The "knock on" impact is hundreds of thousands of decisions to follow Jesus with everyone of them led through water baptism. Further, the multiplier effect includes tens of thousands of new Discipleship Groups, resulting in thousands of new, healthy, multiplying churches and campuses planted.

> Focused Disciple-Making Pastors Develop Strong Disciple-Making Disciples.

All it takes is 10,000 healthy, discipleship-focused Pastors, passionate about equipping and releasing God's people to the mission and ministry God has ordained for them.

- One key is Sabbatical, to get refreshed (& for many this is essential).
- The other is a Strategic Partnership and Plan to get Unstuck and Accelerated in their vision.

Healthy Pastors Develop Healthy Churches

LEARN MORE

Open the QR code and watch a short video which will step you through more of the details.

THE LEADERSCAPE
PODCAST

CLAIM YOUR *FREE* ANNUAL SUBSCRIPTION

FreeAvailOffer.com
To claim your subscription ($59 value)

SCAN HERE TO LEARN MORE

WHAT PEOPLE ARE SAYING ABOUT XLR8

I have known my good friend Michael Murphy to be an astute student, learner, and leader of all things "Church"—its nurturing, development, and growth—both spiritual and strategic. In XLR8, he synthesizes his decades of leadership experience and wisdom and distills it for us to apply to the fulfillment of our own godly vision. I know that every leader who reads this book will want to share its pragmatic wisdom with others. I have learned and grown—you will, too.

—Sam Chand
Leadership Consultant and a friend of Michael Murphy

Mike Murphy understands why Church and church communities matter—for us to be discipled and part of discipling others to impact our families, our communities, and our nation. Mike knows that God's Church is the hope of this side of heaven. XLR8 is not a church growth formula. It is the distilled wisdom of Mike's experience, sacrifice, and passion for making disciples of Christ. Mike's insights are clear, coherent, practical, and humble. They will help church leaders make their churches into what we need them to be.

—Hon. Scott Morrison MP
30th Prime Minister of Australia

In XLR8, Michael Murphy gives you the practical wisdom you need, the encouragement your soul is craving, and the prophetic insight your spirit is crying out for! I know this not just from reading XLR8, but from seeing Michael at work in our church for the past decade! My staff loves him, my Elders value his timely wisdom, and I'm personally grateful to have found a partner like him pushing us forward into church growth.

—Rob Ketterling
Lead Pastor, River Valley Church

Michael Murphy has a unique look at leadership from many vantage points. Serving as Senior Associate Pastor at Hillsong Church, then Senior Pastor of a church in Sydney, Australia, Michael is brilliant at teaching churches around the world the principles that keep them healthy and growing. He has been a great asset to me personally, and I highly recommend his book.

—Steve Kelly
Senior Pastor, Wave Church Virginia Beach, VA

The church has experienced radical change in recent years. Some would term it "disruption". In XLR8, Michael Murphy shares, with his usual enthusiasm, principles he has been teaching leaders around the world for many years, equipping them to fulfill the greatest assignment of all—to make disciples and see the church and the cause of Christ advance.

—Wayne Alcorn
National President, Australian Christian Churches

Michael's vast experience is distilled into compact strategies any church can adopt. Easy to read and applicable to all, *XLR8* will minimize mission drift and benefit every church that puts these principles into practice. Jesus asked us to "make disciples," and this book will help you stay on track.

—*Mark Varughese*
Founder and Senior Leader, Kingdomcity

XLR8 is far more than a book or guide to church strategies and growth but the life work of a man who has lived and breathed every aspect of every page over many decades. Michael Murphy is a role model to every generation of leaders, both on and off the platform. I'm very confident that you will become equipped to build God's house.

—*Joel Cave*
Senior Pastor, Glow Church

Discipleship is one of the secrets of the success of our church; if you want your church to grow, you have to obey the Lord and make disciples! In *XLR8*, Michael helps you do just that. Enjoy!

—*Andrew Corson*
Pastor of "El Lugar de Su Presencia", Bogotá, Colombia

In my journey with countless ministries, few have left an impression on me as deeply as Michael Murphy has. A beacon for the local church, Michael's "Heroes" encapsulates his dedication to faith and community. Each page resonates with tales of unsung heroes, inspiring a profound appreciation for the pillars of our spiritual communities. Michael isn't just an author; he's a dear friend and relentless advocate for the transformative power of the local church. Delve into this masterpiece, and you'll discover the heartbeat of true discipleship.

—*Mr. Steve Chaney, CPA*
Managing Partner, Chaney & Associates: A Professional Corporation

I love Michael Murphy. He is energetic, passionate, engaging, strategic, encouraging, and always looking for his next friend. This book reads like a conversation. You will benefit from his wisdom and passion about the future of your church. I highly recommend that you give it a read.

—*Greg Surratt*
Founding Pastor, Seacoast Church
Co-Founder ARC

Mike Murphy is a man who understands the value and significance of the local church. He is a seasoned leader and brings wisdom that will unlock the potential of many of our churches. Mike is a practical thought leader, and this book provides a clear pathway to achieve greater effectiveness in the development of faith-filled Jesus followers.

—*Phil Dooley*
Global Lead Pastor, Hillsong Church

Michael Murphy is more than a church growth expert; he's a pastor with prophetic mentorship capabilities. Several years ago, over dinner in Queensland, Mike and Val poured into my life at a crucial moment of decision. I know this book will be that same prophetic voice and strategy for every leader with a desire to steward the grace of God on their life well.

—*Nathan Finochio*
Founder of TheosU

For many years, I've watched Michael travel the globe to encourage, and train pastors and leaders. Michael's heart is to help every person he comes in contact with to thrive and grow. This book packages those principles to bring the practical alive and the call of God a reality!

—*Dino Rizzo*
Executive Director of ARC

I can't recommend this book enough! Don't just read it; let it read you and your church. Michael Murphy's humor, insights, heart for the kingdom, and forty years of leadership experience will add value to your world, and I'm praying with him that God will use it to ignite pastors and their teams around the world.

—*Anthony Fleming*
Senior Pastor, Church Alive
President of Transform the Movement

Michael Murphy has been sculpted and molded by God to lead pastors into the realization of their greatest potential and capacity. His mentorship and training caused me to grow my church from 400 to well over 1,100 (and growing) in less than fifteen months. This book contains relevant tools for any ministerial or social context that will produce great church growth and a disciple-making machine!

—*Bishop Jonathan L Woods Snr*
Lead Pastor, All Nations Church
Bishop of Alabama Church of God

In XLR8, Michael Murphy provides a unique and important approach to church health and growth. He successfully blends the practical reality and the spiritual dimension of leading a church congregation to fruitful ministry. The book is not just a manual; it's a source of inspiration. The stories shared will resonate with leaders because of the practical anecdotes and profound insights about leading with authenticity and grace.

—*Stephen Fogarty*
President, Alphacrucis University College

Here's a book that actually works—because it mirrors real life. Michael teaches the exponential power of patterns and processes, but most importantly, he leads us into the expansive landscape of personal growth in Christ. I am deeply grateful that my brother Michael and his wife Valery were faithful to their God-given mission, resilient against all obstacles and willing to sacrifice for the sake of others. From Michael's life and ministry, we have received the tools, roadmap, and inspiration to grow personally and professionally ... and make your dreams come true.

—*Dr. Paul Cole*
President, Christian Men's Network

For as long as I have known Michael Murphy, he has had an unquenchable passion for the church. With practical wisdom and seasoned experience, Michael has written a book that clearly illuminates the path forward for all who see the need for strategic planning to accompany spiritual dynamics in church ministry.

—*Tope Koleoso*
Lead Pastor, Jubilee Church London

This book is hilarious, vulnerable, and chock full of hard-won lessons—with practical, proven strategies. However, the biggest endorsement I can give is that the man who wrote this book is a phenomenal father. He has loved his kids well, held their hands through painful valleys, and been their biggest cheerleader. He's not just a sought-after ministry leader. He is the best Dad in the world. I know because he's mine.

—*Elyse Murphy*
Speaker, Podcaster
One of my favorite preachers (and my youngest daughter!)

I have no idea about all this XLR8 stuff, but he once got twenty parking tickets in six months, which I ended up paying for him. He was the one who broke the window of the local scout hall (though he never admitted it) and gosh, I wish he had tidied his room more. As the eldest of my seven kids, he's a good boy, but someone please tell him to ring his mum more often.

—*Valerie Murphy*
Michael's Mum

Mike is a great friend. He is also a force of nature. His passion and enthusiasm for the church and pastors are, in my opinion, unmatched. Along with this passion are practical insights and systems to help all churches, regardless of size, to take the next step forward into all God has for them.

—*Sean Stanton*
Pastor, Life Unlimited Church and National Secretary Australian Christian Churches

Pastoring and leading the local church over the past few years has not been easy. The "new reality" post-pandemic world has left many leaders discouraged or just plain stuck. I have known Mike Murphy for over three decades, and I have watched him help hundreds of churches get unstuck and dream again. Mike truly is "a pastor's friend". XLR8 reignites our mission to dream again.

—Robert Barriger
Pastor of Camino de Vida, Lima Peru

In XLR8, my friend Michael will not only show you how to double your church's attendance but will also show you how to mobilize your people out of the pews and into the Harvest. If you are ready to put the pedal to the metal and radically expand your Kingdom impact, you have to read this book!

—Josh Howard
Founder, Ignite Movement India

XLR8 serves as an invaluable guide for church leaders, packed with practical strategies and real-life narratives. A magnum opus of over four decades of experience in Christian leadership and a decade of meticulous crafting, Michael's deep insights make it a must-read for any pastors looking to embark on a transformative journey of faith. XLR8 leaps beyond the conventional and brings a fresh perspective as it focuses on unity, truth, engagement, and discipleship with references to finance, stewardship, and generosity. It's not just a book; it's a manual for nurturing a vibrant, engaged, and impactful church.

—Terry Parkman
Generations Director, River Valley Church, MN
OneHope Global NextGen Ambassador & Empowered21
Global NextGen Lead

I believe we are living in a John 21 moment—the greatest catch the world has ever seen is coming! But in order to experience it in our congregations, we need the nets to contain the catch. Too often our nets have tears and we lose the fish—the people—whom the Lord brings to us. In his new book, Michael shares amazing insights and very practical steps based on his years of successful ministry that can help us all prepare our nets so we retain and even multiply the great catch that's coming. I believe this book contains prophetic wisdom that is critical for this time and season we are living in!

—Rabbi Jason Sobel

Copyright © 2023 by Michael R. Murphy

Published by AVAIL

All rights reserved. No portion of this book may be reproduced, stored in a retrieval system, or transmitted in any form or by any means—electronic, mechanical, photocopy, recording, scanning, or other—except for brief quotations in critical reviews or articles, without prior written permission of the author.

Scripture quotations marked KJV are taken from the King James Version of the Bible. Public domain. Scripture quotations marked NIV are taken from the Holy Bible, New International Version®, NIV®. Copyright © 1973, 1978, 1984, 2011 by Biblica, Inc.™ Used by permission of Zondervan. All rights reserved worldwide. www.zondervan.com. The "NIV" and "New International Version" are trademarks registered in the United States Patent and Trademark Office by Biblica, Inc.™ | Scripture quotations marked NKJV are taken from the New King James Version®. Copyright © 1982 by Thomas Nelson. Used by permission. All rights reserved.

For foreign and subsidiary rights, contact the author.

Cover design by Sara Young
Author photo by Andrew James

ISBN: 978-1-962401-15-9   1 2 3 4 5 6 7 8 9 10

Printed in the United States of America

Author's note: Since this book is being published by an American company, they want to use American spelling and punctuation, at least most of the time. To my Aussie colleagues, I'm not sure if I need to say "Forgive me" or "Get over it." Take your pick.